Jane Austen and the North Atlantic

Essays from the 2005 Jane Austen Society
Conference in Halifax, Nova Scotia, Canada

Edited by Sarah Emsley

Jane Austen Society 2006

Acknowledegments

The editor gratefully acknowledges the following for their assistance in the preparation of this volume: Janet Bailey, John Baxter, Lorraine Baxter, Jason Emsley, Sheila Johnson Kindred, and Patrick Stokes.

The cover illustration is from a watercolour drawing of Halifax Harbour in 1846 by Herbert Grey Austen (Private collection).

The Jane Austen Society

Printed by Creative Print & Design 2006

ISBN 0-9538174-7-4

Contents

Address by The Honourable Myra A. Freeman,
Lieutenant Governor of Nova Scotia   5

Introduction   7

Two Naval Brothers, One City: Charles and Francis Austen in Halifax, Canada
Sheila Johnson Kindred   9

Jane Austen and North America: Fact and Fiction
Brian Southam   22

Insular Austen, Oceanic Austen: "Bits of Ivory" and Beyond
Peter W. Graham   38

Canadian and American Readers of Jane Austen's Happy Endings
Sarah Emsley   49

Contributors   61

Address by The Honourable Myra A. Freeman, Lieutenant Governor of Nova Scotia, to the Jane Austen Society at a reception at Government House, September 9, 2005

I am pleased to welcome members of JAS (Jane Austen Society) UK and JASNA (Jane Austen Society of North America) who are in Halifax from September 7-13 to attend a conference on "Jane Austen and the North Atlantic." The conference is, I understand, both a celebration of the associations of Jane Austen's sailor brothers, Charles and Francis, with Halifax and an opportunity to take a look at Jane Austen's writing in the context of the Royal Navy's activities in the North Atlantic and from a North American perspective.

It is pleasing to note how apt Halifax is for this meeting at this time. 2005 is the bicentenary of Charles Austen's maiden voyage to Halifax, the northern base on the North American Station. As you know, he arrived on August 6, 1805 aboard his new sloop of war, HMS Indian, and served for the next six years in the North Atlantic waters cruising south from Halifax. Moreover, this is also the bicentenary of the Battle of Trafalgar, Admiral Nelson's historic victory over the French and Spanish fleets. It is intriguing to realize that Jane Austen's elder brother Sir Francis was one of Nelson's captains. He is also of special interest to Halifax since he subsequently served as Commander-in-Chief of the North American and West Indies Station from 1845-48.

I understand that Jane Austen took a keen interest in her brothers' careers and was highly knowledgeable about the operations of the Royal Navy during the Napoleonic wars. From letters regularly exchanged with both brothers she would have had first-hand accounts of what naval life entailed. It is thought that what she knew from her brothers was particularly important when she came to write her novels *Mansfield Park* and *Persuasion*, both of which contain significant naval characters.

During the conference there will be lectures from Canadian, American, and British academics, some of whom will explore for you the connections of the Austen brothers with Halifax. Many of the places with which they became familiar, both in their professional and social activities, are still standing and in use today. It is most suitable that you will see the Naval Dockyard, the hub of the Austens' working lives while in port, and visit Admiralty House, which was occupied by Admiral Sir Francis Austen while he was station commander. I hope you will be able to take the opportunity to absorb the ambiance of the Georgian buildings that were part of the town Captain Charles Austen knew and that continue to grace the city today. The Austen brothers fulfilled their responsibilities to the Crown in Halifax, but they were also part of the social life of the community. In fact, both sailor brothers were entertained in this very place. For example, 195 years ago Charles Austen and his young wife Fanny enjoyed the hospitality of Government House. In writing home to her sister Esther in Bermuda, a delighted Fanny described "the splendid ball at Government House which we were all at" and where she won $9 at the popular parlour game of Commerce.

Although this afternoon's gathering includes no plans for dancing and gaming, there is a common feature which today's reception shares with that party long ago in 1810. There are Austens at both events! Two direct descendants of Francis Austen, Lt. Cdr. Francis Austen (ret'd) and Belinda Austen, and two direct descendents of Charles Austen, Margaret de Blois Baulch from Australia and Patrick Stokes, Chairman of the Jane Austen Society, are with us today. And to add one more Nova Scotian connection, Margaret Baulch and Patrick Stokes can boast, if they wish, of a Haligonian great grandmother. She was Sophie Emma Deblois, the daughter of Jane Vermilye Pryor and William Minet Deblois. She married Captain Charles Austen's son, Charles John, on September 6, 1848 at St. Paul's Church in Halifax.

I understand that this conference is a special joint meeting of admirers and students of Jane Austen's works from the UK, US, Australia, and Canada and that you chose to hold it in Halifax because of its special associations with Jane Austen's brothers, Charles and Francis. I am delighted that you did so. It is with great pleasure that Nova Scotia welcomes this international gathering to Halifax. I hope you will enjoy your stay in the modern city as you explore the relevance of the older one in the life and work of Jane Austen.

Introduction

Jane Austen never crossed the North Atlantic. Unlike Mrs. Croft in *Persuasion*, who says she has "crossed the Atlantic four times" and travelled "once to the East Indies, ... besides being in different places about home," Austen's personal experience of travel was limited to relatively short journeys such as the ones between Chawton and Godmersham or London. But her brothers, especially Charles and Francis, did travel extensively, and through her knowledge of their journeys, her experience of the pleasures and difficulties of short trips, and her imaginative engagement with the idea of what it means to travel away from home and back again, Jane Austen explored both the familiar and the unfamiliar. The four papers presented at the 2005 Jane Austen Society Conference in Halifax, Nova Scotia, and collected in this volume analyze the literal journeys of Charles and Francis Austen, some of the imagined journeys and naval experiences in Jane Austen's novels, and a range of transatlantic responses to her fictional world.

Reading these fresh perspectives on "Jane Austen and the North Atlantic" expands our knowledge of Austen family biography and extends our understanding of the size, scope, and effects of Austen's novels. Reproduced here in the order in which they were presented at the Conference, the papers move from fact toward fiction, beginning with the history of Jane Austen's brothers in Halifax and concluding with a discussion of her fictional endings. In "Two Naval Brothers, One City: Charles and Francis Austen in Halifax, Canada," Sheila Johnson Kindred provides what she calls a "biographic snapshot" of the time the brothers spent on the North American Station, using new research from North American and British archival sources to illuminate the story. Brian Southam, in "Jane Austen and North America: Fact and Fiction," describes the Austen family connections with both Bermuda and Nova Scotia, highlighting relevant passages from Jane Austen's letters and drawing parallels between the experiences of Charles and Francis Austen and their sister's depiction of naval life in *Mansfield Park* and *Persuasion*.

Peter W. Graham's "Insular Austen, Oceanic Austen: 'Bits of Ivory' and Beyond" analyzes the apparent tension between the narrow geographic and social focus of Jane Austen's novels and the broader context of critical interpretations as well as of what he calls "diverse fictive or cinematic borrowings, extensions, or recontextualizations" of her work. Finally, my own essay on "Canadian and American Readers of Jane Austen's Happy Endings" discusses some of the ways in which the novels may be seen as therapeutic and stresses the connection between Austen's happy endings and the theological virtue of hope.

One of the conference lectures, Brian Cuthbertson's "Halifax: Then and Now," does not appear in this collection because it was an illustrated oral history of Halifax, rather than a formal paper. Interested readers may wish to consult Cuthbertson's fine books on Nova Scotia history, especially *The Halifax Citadel: Portrait of a Military Fortress* (Halifax, NS: Formac, 2001).

Conference attendees were fortunate to be invited to a reception at Government House (the oldest Vice-Regal residence in Canada), home of Her Honour the Honourable Myra A. Freeman, Lieutenant Governor of Nova Scotia, and her husband, His Honour Lawrence A. Freeman. Their Honours offered a warm welcome to JAS and JASNA members, and in this volume we are pleased to include the text of Her Honour's address to the assembled group of Jane Austen admirers and members of the Austen family.

Thanks to the efforts of the Jane Austen Society, under the excellent leadership of Patrick Stokes and supported by the Halifax chapter of the Jane Austen Society of North America, the imaginative idea of bringing together Canadian, American, and British speakers, along with participants from JAS and JASNA (including members from Australia, Japan), was realized and the 2005 Halifax Conference lived up to its motto of "Hands across the sea."

Sarah Emsley
Cambridge, Massachusetts
March 2006

Two Naval Brothers, One City:
Charles and Francis Austen in Halifax, Canada
Sheila Johnson Kindred

Jane Austen was well aware of Halifax, Nova Scotia. We know this because she mentioned the town in her correspondence with Cassandra. On April 11, 1805 Jane told her sister of a recently completed letter she expected to be carried by the *Urania* which was "joining the convoy to Halifax" (*Letters*, 11 April 1805). It was addressed to her younger brother Charles, newly posted across the Atlantic, and is one she had taken some pains to create, bestowing on it a generous portion of her "wit and leisure." Six years later, Jane shared with Cassandra in another letter that "on the authority of some other captain from Halifax," Charles was "bringing the *Cleopatra* home" (*Letters*, 25 April 1811). These references to Halifax by Jane are notable markers of the beginning and end of Charles's service at sea on the North American Station. But what is known about his time here? As it happens, little has been written about Charles's years in North America or his visits to Halifax, the northern hub of the station.[1] Yet these were important years for Charles's naval career: he was on his first command, he would be made post captain in 1810 and he was able to enjoy the pursuit of naval prize and its profits.

I will tell you shortly about Charles's early career seen through the lens of his sojourns in Halifax, but first let me introduce the other naval Austen. The family's connection with this city came full circle when, 28 years after her death, Jane's elder brother, Vice Admiral Sir Francis Austen was appointed Commander-in-Chief of the North American and West Indies Station, a post he held from 1845 until 1848. Now, in 2005, the bicentenary of the younger brother Charles's first arrival in Halifax, it is most appropriate to explore aspects of both Charles's and Francis's careers which relate to this city. This, then, is a tale of two naval brothers in the one city – Halifax. It's a story about their experiences, their personalities and the nature of naval service during the turbulent times of the Napoleonic wars and the peace that followed.

Charles John Austen: Commander and Post Captain

During Charles's service on the North American Station the political climate was particularly tense. England was at war with France and the Royal Navy's strategy was to contain the French fleet and prevent supplies from reaching France and her allies. At the same time the Navy had to ensure that essential goods reached England. Given this situation, the assignments of the North American Squadron included seeking the recovery of deserters from British warships, cruising for trade protection, blockading American trade with Napoleonic Europe, escorting convoys of troops, mastships and merchant men, and patrolling the coast from Nova Scotia waters to "as far south as Florida and ranging well east, north, and south of Bermuda"

(Gwyn 128). Nor was the French war the only cause for concern. Relations with the United States were increasingly unsettled, especially after 1807, the year *HMS Leopard* (50 guns) mounted an unprovoked attack on the unsuspecting American frigate *US Chesapeake* (76 guns) over the question of deserters.

From Charles's perspective his public duties must have seemed routine and repetitive. Most of the squadron's vessels, including his, were undermanned and often staffed by unmotivated seamen who had been pressed into service. In this situation, one did the best job one could while at sea. Conceivably, when he was at the northern end of the station, it was a welcome break to come into Halifax. Here, a captain could ensure his vessel was in good working order, stock up with provisions for the next assignment, do any private business and enjoy the company of fellow officers and the upper classes of Halifax society.

Charles brought his newly built 400 ton, 18 gun sloop of war *Indian* into Halifax, on her maiden voyage from Bermuda, on August 6, 1805.[2] After a general inspection at the Naval Yard, *Indian* was at sea and at work. Charles was clearly proud of his vessel and keen to keep it in ship shape, for *Indian*'s log books carefully record many instances of the comprehensive repairs and refits taking place in the Naval Yard. For example, during a major refit in autumn 1809, the log is peppered with references to the great variety of requirements of a sailing sloop of war. Here are just a few examples: "Unbent the sails and sent them ashore to the Dockyard" (15 September); "Readying her for heaving down, transported ship to the Careening Wharf"[3] (1, 2 November); and "Rattling down the Top Mast Rigging" (7 November) (ADM 51/1991). Also at the Naval Yard were considerable naval stores from which Charles could provision *Indian* prior to a cruise and acquire any necessary ordinance.

The Naval Yard was pivotal to Charles and the squadron's safety, for as naval historian Julian Gwyn has observed, their extensive cruising took "a heavy toll on the masts, yards, sails and rigging, and when ships struck a ledge or a shoal on their copper bottoms" (Gwyn 129). Until greatly improved dockyard facilities were developed in Bermuda in 1809 and after, the squadron depended on the services and skills uniquely available in Halifax. Charles was to be particularly grateful for the Naval Yard's expertise when, in July 1808, *Indian* urgently needed her ballast increased and rebalanced. Otherwise, she would have been in danger when working off a lea shore because she could not have carried a sufficient quantity of sail.

Charles's satisfaction in putting his ship in order contrasts sharply with his apparent displeasure when required to participate in a court martial. While in harbour in 1809, Charles had first-hand experience of such judicial proceedings. A court martial was held on *HMS Pompee* to rule in the case brought against mutineers and deserters belonging to HMS *Columbine*. *Indian*'s log tersely records that "at 7:30 came alongside Jas Jackson and Tho's Hearne [who] received 30 lashes each according to sentence of Court Martial" (20 September 1809). In the course of being flogged round the fleet, each man was to receive the horrific total of 500 lashes. Subsequently Jackson and Hearne were classed as convicts and banished for seven years.

That Charles found the violence and brutality implicit in such punishments upsetting can be surmised from his observations in later years. In a private journal written in 1826 Charles observed: "Went aboard the *Magnificent* before 8am [for a court martial] after which the captain assembled and I presided for the first time and did not acquit myself to my satisfaction" (13 December). When Charles returned to the proceedings three days later he felt "very weak afterwards." It is with noticeable relief that he records the court martial was "finished at last to my great joy by 11am" (AUS/120).

As well as his public duties while in Halifax, Charles had a measure of interesting private business. Halifax was the site of a Vice Admiralty court and Charles retained a prize agent, the wealthy and canny merchant Andrew Belcher, whose job was to look after his client's interests before the court and at the auction houses. Charles was involved in naval prize taking between 1805 and 1808, for during this period he was party to the seizure of thirteen vessels. Some of these were solo captures; others were made in the company of additional ships from the squadron.[4] On four particular occasions Charles and his co-captors detained at sea two foreign vessels and two American merchantmen together with their apparently illicit cargoes. These prizes were sent to Halifax for adjudication. In the case of the Spanish Schooner *Rosalie* and her cargo, the Swedish ship *Dygden* and her cargo and part of the cargo of the American ship *Ocean*, Justice Croke's court ruled in favour of Charles and his co-captors (NAC: RG8 IV). Thus, they became the happy recipients of one quarter of the proceeds of the sale of the vessels and cargoes at auction, less fees and costs. His officers and men claimed a lesser share.[5]

This involvement in naval prize gave Charles's Halifax visits an added interest. He had the satisfaction of conferring, when possible, with his agent Andrew Belcher, and thus discovering how his prize cases were progressing before the courts. Both *Rosalie* and *Ocean* actually paid out when he was in port here. Such windfalls were most welcome for an officer whose salary was about 200 pounds per year. Yet Charles also knew first-hand about the gambles and pitfalls of prize taking. Though Justice Croke had found the American ship *Sally* to be "good and lawful prize," the Court of Appeal in England reversed this decision (NA: HCA 46/8). Consequently, a somewhat poorer Charles and his co-captor Captain Edward Hawker were jointly responsible for legal and associated costs incurred during prolonged court proceedings. Even worse, they had to abandon any expectations they had earlier had regarding the nearly four thousand pounds already realized by the sale of *Sally* and her cargo.

Not all of Charles's pursuits in Halifax were solely of a professional or financial nature. On a lighter note, the town offered him opportunities for sociability and relaxation, both presumably welcome options after weeks at sea. But what sort of town was it? And who would he choose to meet while ashore?

From one perspective, Halifax was a typical, busy seaport town with a thriving waterfront. Yet, close by existed pockets of squalor and vice. On Barracks Street, just under the Citadel, scores of taverns and brothels did a lively trade, patronized regularly by inebriated sailors and other assorted life. Fear frequently surfaced among the working classes when the hated press gangs stormed through the streets collecting up unwilling "recruits" for enforced naval service. Moreover, even in the midst of war-time prosperity, one quarter of the population in the year 1810-1811 subsisted on food and firewood distributed for the relief of the destitute. This poorer, meaner town was not the Halifax Charles would seek to know. He mixed with the Halifax of the professional, government, administrative and wealthy merchant classes.[6] These were the people of ambition, education and genteel habits; they liked to live well and were anxious to show themselves off to advantage. Into this prosperous milieu, naval officers were in constant demand, frequently invited and warmly welcomed.

Jane Austen's letters give the impression that Charles was very personable and naturally convivial. "A ball" she once observed to Cassandra, would be a "likely spot to find a Charles" (*Letters*, 8-9 November 1800). Presumably, however, Charles chose his social occasions depending on both his own inclinations and his marital status. On arrival in 1805, he was a dashing, handsome, young captain, just the sort of fine naval figure some Halifax girl would willingly set her cap at. In fact, local newspapers record scores of weddings taking place between Halifax girls and naval officers during Charles's time on the station, including the nuptials of two titled fellow officers, Lord James Townshend and the Hon. Henry Dilkes Byng. However, Charles was not in this market as he had fallen in love and married in May 1807 the young Fanny Fitzwilliam Palmer, daughter of John Grove Palmer, Attorney General of Bermuda.

It would be intriguing to know where he actually went and who he saw while in Halifax. Speculative though it is, an educated guess is possible, thanks to a letter by Samuel Hood George, the young secretary to Lt. Gov. George Prevost, to his mother. It reads: "For the next week we are to have nothing but gaiety. Tomorrow [18 October 1809] we dine at the Commissioner's [Captain John Inglefield of the Naval Yard] who is the gaiest of the gay and in the evening we go on board Sir Alexander Cochrane's ship *Pompee,* to a Ball and supper, on Friday to Mrs. Belcher's party,[7] on Monday a play, on Tuesday a dinner given by the merchants to Sir Alexander Cochrane and so we pass our time" (SHG 244, 17). *Indian*'s log establishes that Charles was in port this very week awaiting the completion of his vessel's refit. As he was known personally to Commissioner Inglefield, Admiral Cochrane, and the Belchers, we can readily imagine that Charles was of the party for some of these festivities.

Charles loved the theatre and no doubt frequented Halifax's Theatre Royal. The theatre, located on Argyle Street near St. Paul's Church, was under the supervision of professional actor and director Charles Stewart Powell. The Theatre Royal offered a diverse repertoire[8] and had even included performances of *Lovers' Vows* during July and August of 1806 (RNSG 2 July 1806). What a pity that Charles was then at sea and thus missed, by a fortnight, a chance to see the very play that Jane Austen would later make central to the plot of *Mansfield Park*.

During Charles's last year on the station a particularly memorable professional duty brought him to Halifax. He arrived on May 27, 1810 on *HMS Swiftsure* (50 guns) carrying a distinguished passenger, Vice Admiral Sir John Borlase Warren, his Commander-in-Chief on the station, together with the Admiral's retinue. The party included Charles's wife Fanny, their one-and-a-half-year-old daughter Cassandra and the redoubtable Lady Warren, wife of Sir John.

Charles's recent promotion from *Indian* to become flag captain of *HMS Swiftsure* had been completely unexpected. It had occurred because *Swiftsure*'s captain, John Conn, was tragically drowned just days before. While cruising just off Bermuda in early May, Conn, according to newspaper reports, "fell out of the cabin window, having, it is supposed, overreached himself while observing some painting that had been done to the stern of the ship" (RNSG 20 May 1810). "Not withstanding every exertion made to save him [Conn] perished" (WC 1 June 1810). In consequence, Warren immediately needed a flag captain. To the Austens' great joy, he chose Charles, making him post captain in the bargain.[9] This promotion was absolutely crucial for Charles's career because, given the naval regulations of the time, his future advancement henceforth depended only on his seniority in active service.

Since Charles had been married since 1807, his personal life and pursuits were shared with Fanny whenever his naval duties allowed them to be together. In the summer of 1810, Fanny's letters from Halifax to her sister Esther in Bermuda provide a unique perspective on the social and naval world she was then enjoying with Charles. There are reports of Lady Prevost's "splendid ball [at Government House] which we were all at" and where Fanny won $9 at Commerce, a popular parlour game which involved barter (Letters, 12 June 1810). On another occasion, "all the great people dined at the Rockingham Club," while the ladies, including Lady Prevost and Lady Warren, "had a very pleasant evening at Mrs. Belcher's (Birch Cove). The gentlemen joined us in the evening and escorted us home" (Letters, 17 June 1810). "It was very agreeable," reported the evidently delighted Fanny, who had earlier observed that "Lady Warren and the Admiral are both extremely kind and attentive to me and are very fond of my little Cassy" (Letters, 12 June 1810).

Apart from their professional and social obligations in Halifax,[10] Charles and Fanny had time for themselves together with their young daughter, Cassandra. A child whose mother described her as "so riotous and unmanageable that I can do nothing with her" (Letters, 1 June 1810) may be considered something of a mixed blessing. However, they were all united in Halifax for over two months in 1810. This was important in itself, as Charles's career had so often separated him from his family.

Yet this was not the first time the Austens had been together in Halifax. Fanny and baby Cassandra had been with him during the previous autumn when *Indian* was in port from September 14 to November 29, 1809 for extensive repairs. During that time the young couple made a significant decision: they had their daughter christened. St. Paul's church records show that Cassandra, age 10 months, was baptized on October 6, 1809. This is very surprising, especially as Charles wrote his sister Cassandra on Christmas Day, 1808 to proudly report the safe arrival of his first born whom he "means to call Cassandra Esten" and to ask his sister to "to be a sponsor" of the child. According to Charles, he is "interrupted by Mr. Depassau who is going to baptise the children but as they are not quite made up [he] has consented to eat cake and drink some wine" (Letter to Cassandra, 25 December 1808). These communications suggest that a Bermuda baptism was imminent, which would have been a very appropriate decision. Fanny's family was at hand, her sister Esther had just given birth on December 12 and the Rev. Mr. Depassau, the vicar of St. Peter's Church in St. Georges, Bermuda, had married Fanny and Charles the year before. However, the entry in the church registry establishes a very different state of affairs.

The puzzle is why Fanny and Charles would choose Halifax for the baptism of their child. Something during their stay must have motivated them to ask the Rev. Robert Stanser, rector of St. Paul's and chaplain to the Royal Navy, to christen their child. And although the baby's aunt Cassandra would not be able to attend, the other sponsor, Captain Edward Hawker, had just arrived from a cruise and so presumably he would have helped make this event a memorable occasion.

There does remain a visual souvenir of the Austens' visits to Halifax. While in port Charles arranged for Halifax-based British artist Robert Field to paint a small head and shoulders portrait of himself. It depicts a handsome young captain whose expression is both engaging and sympathetic. Most probably, this portrait was commissioned to mark Charles's promotion to post captain in 1810. Maybe it was also a special gift for Fanny so she could constantly have his likeness with her when he was away at sea.

Happy though their Halifax sojourn of 1810 was, there was a keen disappointment at its close. In August the *Swiftsure* had transported the 1st battalion of the 7th Fusiliers to Portugal to join British regiments already fighting in the Peninsular War. On Charles's return in September, he found the now Admiral Warren on the verge of retirement and learned of his own removal into the frigate *Cleopatra* (32 guns). Although he had dreamed of commanding a frigate, this reality was short lived. As the Admiralty in London did not confirm his appointment, he brought the *Cleopatra* home with the convoy in July of 1811, and then left her for good. By November Samuel John Pechell was appointed her captain. A colleague of Charles's on the station and someone described enthusiastically by Fanny as "my very great favourite Captain Pechell" (Letters, 14 August 1810), he was also the nephew of the forceful Lady Warren. Clearly, Pechell had avenues of influence that Charles did not.

In sum, what did Halifax mean to Charles? It was a safe harbour and a base which provided the means to maintain his "beloved" *Indian* and his later vessels *Swiftsure* and *Cleopatra*; it was the location of the Vice Admiralty Court, whose judgements about naval prize brought him some welcome financial gain. Finally, Halifax was a place to savour his new status of flag captain and post captain, somewhere to relax, to socialize and a place where on several occasions he shared both his professional and personal life with his adored wife, Fanny, and their little daughter.

Sir Francis William Austen: Vice Admiral of the White: Commander-in-Chief of the North American and West Indies Station

Sir Francis's tenure on the North American Station began 34 years later during a period of peace and relative prosperity. He was 71 years of age and beginning his last active service at sea. His flag ship, the impressive 50 gun *HMS Vindictive*, was one of a squadron of 13 under his command. Ten of these vessels navigated by sail and the remaining three were additionally equipped to use steam. For three years beginning in 1845, *Vindictive* and the squadron made their headquarters in Halifax from June to late October. While based here, Sir Francis deployed his squadron to ensure the protection of the fisheries against American interests, to make coastal surveys, and to maintain a British presence in colonial waters.

Vice Admiral Austen first arrived in Halifax on *HMS Vindictive* on June 19, 1845, where, according to the local press, "he disembarked under a salute from the Citadel and was received with a guard of honour on landing" (*Morning Chronicle* 19 June 1845). Once on site he set about his administrative tasks with rigour and precision. His comprehensive *General Instructions and Port Orders for the Squadron Employed on the North America and West India Station* (GO) convey the tenor of his command. Given aboard the *Vindictive*, at Halifax, July 1, 1845, these orders stipulate in great detail what is expected of the ships, their officers and men in matters of refitting, provisioning, ordinance, navigation, safety, discipline, and general behaviour. Although some of its contents may simply reflect what was required by the Navy irrespective of the station, this document was written in Sir Francis's own words and seems to capture the tone of his priorities during his command.

As they apply to Halifax, several directives are of particular interest. For example, Sir Francis's orders show concern not only for the safety of the squadron but also for others in distress. He stipulated that "whenever the Signals for Vessels being in distress at the entrance of the Harbour shall be hoisted on Citadel Hill, assistance is to be immediately sent from each Ship. A Launch, with an Anchor and Hawser, is always to be kept in readiness for that purpose at one of the Wharfs of the Yard" (GO 3, 51).

Sir Francis was particularly innovative regarding the health of his men. While in port in 1846, he introduced the notion of a temporary hospital for "patients employed in the northern part of the station during the summer months." Using part of the old naval hospital and the services of *Vindictive*'s surgeon and her medical supplies made it possible to care for patients in a setting more conducive to recovery (AUS/11 22 June 1846). Another commitment to healthy practices is his directive forbidding the dumping of waste. Speaking as an early environmentalist, he required that "whenever any Ship may have occasion to go alongside the Wharf at Halifax Yard, care is to be taken to prevent any rubbish or dirt from being thrown overboard" (GO 2, 51).

By this time steam vessels made up about one quarter of the navy's complement and Sir Francis's squadron included steam sloops *Vesuvius*, *Columbia*, and *Hermes*. As it turned out, the machinery of the steam vessels often presented specific operational problems. Sir Francis was quick to trouble-shoot and recommend solutions. For instance, he issued specific cautions against getting steam up too fast, about economizing on fuel and the necessity of employing competent stokers for the boilers (GO 4, 49).

According to Bermuda historian Henry Wilkinson, Sir Francis "attended to his official duties scrupulously but was little concerned with ... the lighter aspects of social life" (Wilkinson 569-70). Certainly at his age and given his somewhat serious temperament, it is understandable why he did not particularly seek the company of local society or desire to host formal balls and dinners at his official residences in Halifax and Bermuda beyond what was necessary. As it was, he already enjoyed the company of his "family ship" which included sons George, the chaplain, Herbert Grey, flag lieutenant, his nephew Charles John Austen, flag lieutenant, and his two unmarried daughters Cassandra and Frances. His son Herbert Grey was the "little Herbert" of Jane Austen's letters, to whom she had "sent her love" on the occasion of his birth (*Letters*, 24 November 1815). This intimate group was Sir Francis's coterie, though Cassandra's charms are questionable, as her allegedly imperious and strident manner had earned her the sobriquet of "Miss Vindictive" among some shipboard circles (Southam 320).

By appointing his son Herbert Grey first to the post of flag lieutenant and subsequently to be commander of the steam vessel *Vesuvius*, Sir Francis created a vacancy on *Vindictive*, which he conveniently filled with his nephew Charles John, son of his naval brother Charles. In so doing Francis acted benevolently with the advancement of his family's careers in mind. These placements also made possible certain personal projects. Herbert Grey, as was his wont wherever he was posted, took sketch pad and watercolours and vividly recorded his impression of the place where he was. His cousin, Charles John, did something even more romantic. He fell in love and subsequently married a young Halifax girl, Sophie Emma Deblois at St. Paul's Church on September 6, 1848.[11]

Due to Herbert's artistic skills, we have the privilege and pleasure of seeing Halifax, its harbour and environs as he saw them. This artistic legacy is valuable in itself, for Herbert had a fine sense of design and a very good eye for colour. But his watercolours are also of interest for their informative content, as they bring to life the very settings in which *Vindictive* and *Vesuvius* served on the station. As it turned out Herbert Austen was not the only artist on board *Vindictive*. Flag captain

Michael Seymour had similar interests and the two officers no doubt often sketched together. Seymour's very specific titles locate quite precisely some of the places where the men positioned themselves. For example, Seymour's sketches include "Halifax from McNab's Island, 25 August, 1845" and "Admiralty House from the flag ship *Vindictive*'s mooring, 19 June 1845."[12]

Vice Admiral Francis Austen's nephew Charles John had joined *Vindictive* as flag lieutenant by February of 1847. Perhaps it was that summer that he met his Sophie. Her family were prominent and highly successful Halifax merchants. From Loyalist stock on both the Deblois and Pryor sides of her family, she was one of nine children born to Jane Vermilye Pryor and William Minet Deblois. Her grandmother, Sarah Deblois, had the distinction of being one of the very first woman merchants in Nova Scotia, when she took over and ran her husband George's commercial concerns after his sudden death in 1799. In fact, Sarah was in business and advertising the sale of exotic teas, such as "Bohea, Hyson and Souchong" when Charles Austen first arrived on the station in 1805. Who knows? They may have even done business together, not knowing that an important link would be forged between their families over forty years later! As it is, all the living descendents of Jane Austen's brother Charles come from this union of his son with Sophie Emma. In consequence, they are part Nova Scotian themselves.[13]

Conclusion

In writing this account of the Austen naval brothers' time in Halifax, I have employed the device of empathetic imagination. I have searched naval records, read letters written by Jane Austen, Fanny Austen and Charles Austen, combed through contemporary newspapers and the *Naval Chronicle*. I have explored vice admiralty court records and consulted the findings of several naval historians. With the facts I have discovered I have tried to draw a biographic snapshot of the lives and times of Charles and Francis Austen while at the Halifax end of the North American Station.

There is a sense in which Jane Austen herself was also a constructor of biography. We know that she was vitally interested in the careers of her sailor brothers, so how might she have accessed the essentials of Charles's naval service in North America? Contemporary newspapers and the biannual *Naval Chronicle* reported the navy's activities in some detail. Additionally, *Steel's Naval Lists*, the very source consulted by Anne Elliot in *Persuasion,* would make Jane familiar with the logistics of naval manoeuvres, postings, promotions and the composition of the squadrons assigned to each station. Then, of course, there was all the correspondence among members of the Austen family. Although the letters between Charles and Jane for this period are missing, what else would he have written to her about if not the size and state of his vessels, the luck and logistics of naval prize taking, the various vice admirals commanding the station and their wives, the friendships among his fellow officers, his own little family, his professional advancement, and much more?

So, Jane Austen had at hand all the right sort of materials from which she could construct her own "biography" of Charles for the period he was away. This process would be personally satisfying for a sister so attached to a younger brother. But there were additional benefits for Jane from an artistic point of view. In the course of reconstructing Charles's life experiences, she would have incidentally acquired the kind of insights about naval life which would have stood her in good stead when she later came to create such memorable naval characters as Frederick Wentworth, his brother officers, and Admiral Croft in *Persuasion* and William Price in *Mansfield Park*. At the time when Jane Austen was communicating with Charles on the North American Station, she may not have suspected that information about her brother's time in Halifax would ever influence her artistically, but it is a pleasure to think that their correspondence quite likely did.

Works Cited

Published Sources

Austen, Francis W. *General Instructions and Port Orders for the Squadron Employed on the North America and West India Station*. Halifax, NS: Gossip and Coade, 1845.

Austen, Jane. *Jane Austen's Letters*. Ed. Deirdre LeFaye. Oxford: OUP, 1997.

Austen-Leigh, William and Richard Arthur; revised and enlarged by Deirdre LeFaye. *Jane Austen: A Family Record*. London: GK Hall/MacMillan, 1989.

Gwyn, Julian. *Frigates and Foremasts: The North American Squadron in Nova Scotia Waters 1745-1815*. Vancouver, BC: University of British Columbia Press, 2004.

---. *Ashore and Afloat: The British Navy and the Halifax Naval Dockyard before 1820*. Ottawa, ON: University of Ottawa Press, 2004.

Kindred, Sheila Johnson. "Charles Austen: Prize Chaser and Prize Taker on the North American Station 1805-1808." *Persuasions* 26 (2004): 188-194.

Notman, Suzanne. "Fanny Austen's Letters." *The Bermudian*. March, 2000.

Southam, Brian. *Jane Austen and the Navy*. 2nd edition. Greenwich, London: National Maritime Museum, 2005.

---. "Jane Austen's Sailor Brothers: Francis and Charles in Life and Art." *Persuasions* 25 (2003): 33-45.

Vincent, Thomas B. "The Inquisition: Alexander Croke's Satire on Halifax Society during the Wentworth Years." *The Dalhousie Review* 53.3 (1973): 404-430.

Wilkinson, Henry. *Bermuda from Sail to Steam: The History of the Island from 1784-1901*. 2 vol. London: OUP, 1973.

Unpublished Sources

Admiralty Papers (ADM). National Archives (NA). Kew, London, England.

Austen, Charles John. Papers (AUS/120). National Maritime Museum (NMM). Greenwich, London, England.

Austen, Charles John. Letter to Cassandra Austen, 25 December 1808. Pierpont Morgan Library. New York, NY. Manuscript 4500.

Austen, Francis William. Papers (AUS/11). NMM.

Austen, Fanny. Letters to Esther Esten. Pierpont Morgan Library. New York, NY. Manuscript 4500.

George, Samuel Hood. Letters (SHG). George Papers. Nova Scotia Archives and Record Management (NSARM). Halifax, NS.

Halifax Vice Admiralty Court Records 1805-1808. RG8 IV. National Archives of Canada (NAC). Ottawa, ON.

Morning Chronicle, 1845. NSARM. Halifax, NS.

Royal Nova Scotia Gazette, 1805-1810 (RNSG). NSARM. Halifax, NS.

Weekly Chronicle, 1805-1810 (WC). NSARM. Halifax, NS.

Notes

1 In *Jane Austen and the Navy*, 2nd edition, Brian Southam makes some reference to Charles's naval service on the North American Station during 1805-1811. See 53-54, 136, 268. See also his article "Jane Austen's Sailor Brothers: Francis and Charles in Life and Art" 37, 38. Much briefer mention occurs in *Jane Austen: A Family Record*. The authors note in passing that "since 1804 [Charles] had been engaged in the unpleasant and unprofitable task of enforcing the right of search on the Atlantic seaboard of America, to ensure that neutral countries such as America were not trading with France" (143). A useful source for Fanny Austen's visit to Halifax is Suzanne Notman's article "Fanny Austen's Letters."
2 Apart from the reference to a complement of 20 guns in Charles Austen's recruitment notice (see Southam), there are varying references to *Indian*'s ordinance. A number of naval sources rate her as an 18 gun sloop of war. Steel's *List of the Royal Navy* describes her as an 18 gun vessel which sometimes carried 24 guns.

3 The careening wharf was a facility where a vessel could be turned on her side in order to clean, caulk or repair the exposed side of her bottom.
4 For an overview of Charles's involvement with naval prize, including those captures adjudicated at Bermuda, see Sheila Johnson Kindred, "Charles Austen: Prize Chaser and Prize Taker on the North American Station 1805-1808."
5 Prize shares were distributed according to an established formula. Prior to June 1808, the captain received a two eighth share, the flag officer or admiral received one eighth, one eighth went to the masters and lieutenants, another eighth to the warrant sea officers, a further eighth to the inferior and petty officers, and the remaining quarter to the crew and marines. See Southam, *Jane Austen and the Navy* 123. In the case of joint captures, the captain's share was divided among the participating captains.
6 There is a biting satirical poem from this period entitled "The Inquisition," which speaks to the gaiety, foibles and moral misadventures of the Halifax upper classes. Written by Justice Croke of the Vice Admiralty Court, it was clandestinely in circulation in 1805, just as Charles was arriving on the station. Croke, though highly competent in legal matters, had been socially ostracized by the majority of the Halifax upper classes. As one commentator on the poem has remarked: "[Croke] seemed to have a special knack of enraging those with whom he dealt" and in consequence presumably "lost some of the delicate balance between moral objectivity and personal vengeance when his wrote his poem" (Vincent 406). However, irrespective of Croke's soundness as a judge of character, his descriptions of festivities are very charming. For example, at the planning of a ball: "Cards fly by packs to folks of each degree, / Request the favour, and the RSVP / ...What Turkies, Chickens, Pigs and Pidgeons fell / To grace the banquet, not the Muse could tell" (ll.57-58; 61-62). And on the day of the ball: "The Dames arrive in Muslins, Gauzes, Satins / In Chariots, One Horse Chaise and Pattens / ...The gaudy banners flutter to the Air, / The Silver Side board groans with sumptuous fare / The fiddles crash, the merry Tabours beat / In Notes responsive to the dancers' feet" (ll. 65-66; 69-72). Tom Vincent's article "The Inquisition: Alexander Croke's Satire on Halifax Society during the Wentworth Years" includes the text of the poem.
7 Marianne Belcher was the aunt of Captain Marryat, who became famous for naval novels such as *Peter Simple* and *Mr. Midshipman Easy*. Marryat arrived on the station, joining *HMS Aeolus* as a lieutenant, just as Charles was leaving for England.
8 During occasions that Charles was in Halifax, the playbills for the Theatre Royal were advertised in the *Royal Nova Scotia Gazette*. They included: *The Wheel of Fortune*, a comedy; *Neck or Nothing*, a farce (6 September 1808); *Douglas*, a tragedy (31 October 1809); and *The Foundling of the Forest*, a comedy (15 May 1811).
9 Upon returning to Bermuda fifteen years later, Charles was moved with emotion

when, at St. John's Hill, he "looked at the Admiral's House in which I had not been since the day Sir John Warren told me he had made me a Post Captain in poor John Conn's vacancy" (Diary, 20 July 1826).

10 As Charles had earlier joined the Masonic Lodge in Bermuda, his brother Masons would have welcomed his participation while in Halifax. However, on this occasion his chances for involvement were somewhat thwarted as Fanny, in the rush of departure, had failed to pack his Masonic apron, an item which she requested her sister Esther in Bermuda to search for and send (Letters, 17 June 1810).

11 While contemporary references in Halifax records preserve the "Deblois" spelling, alternative spellings of this family name are on record.

12 PowerPoint images of a selection of watercolour sketches of Halifax harbour and environs by Lt. Herbert Grey Austen and Capt. Michael Seymour accompanied the delivery of this paper at the conference.

13 The conference was attended by two direct descendents of Charles John Austen: Patrick Stokes, conference organizer and Chairman of JAS, and his sister Margaret Baulch and by two direct descendents of Admiral Sir Francis Austen: Lt. Cdr. Francis Austen (ret'd) and Belinda Austen.

Jane Austen and North America: Fact and Fiction
Brian Southam

Of all English novelists, Jane Austen is the most assuredly English, the one English novelist who stayed at home, whose only sea voyage was the few miles to the Isle of Wight. She is famously the novelist who never left the territory of England, not even to visit Scotland or Wales. Her writing carries this insularity to the last degree. Not a page takes us outside her native country. Abroad is sometimes talked about but never travelled to. The foreigner is an absent species. Her scenes and characters are set firmly in the country houses and small towns of Southern England, with occasional visits to London and Bath, and one trip North, to Derbyshire, when Elizabeth Bennet pays her fateful visit to Darcy's home at Pemberley, in the Peak district, not two hundred miles from London.

It may seem bizarre, therefore, to connect Jane Austen with North America. Exactly the same question arose five years ago when the Society held an earlier Conference in Bermuda. What had Jane Austen to do with these places? The connecting link, of course, is in the travels of her sailor brothers, Francis and Charles. Between them, they sailed much of the world. For Charles in particular, the Bermuda-Halifax connection covers perhaps the most important phase of his life. In 1804, at the age of the age of 25, Charles was promoted to the rank of Commander to captain a small vessel, the *Indian*, then being built in Bermuda, and in the following year it was in this ship that he made his first voyage to Halifax. This was the beginning of his six-and-a-half years' service in the North America Command, a tour of duty which was to bring him to Halifax at least once a year, sometimes more, staying there for weeks at a time, sometimes a couple of months;[1] a tour of duty which also saw him promoted to Captain and married to a Bermuda bride. Francis, too, had his connections with North America and the North America Command. So while Halifax and Bermuda were geographically remote from Jane Austen's England, they were brought home to her through the experiences of the sailor brothers, experiences which she drew upon in writing her 'naval' novels, *Mansfield Park* and *Persuasion*.

*

Although the first biography of Jane Austen – the *Memoir of Jane Austen*, published in 1870 – does not have anything at all to say on these matters (neither Halifax nor Bermuda is mentioned), it is quite invaluable in giving us an insider's view, coming as it does from someone who knew Jane Austen personally, a nephew, James Edward Austen-Leigh. One of the things that strikes the reader immediately is the emphasis that Austen-Leigh places on the naval aspect of her writing and her affection for the service. This is a subject which he places, very deliberately, in the early pages of the book, referring there to what he calls his Aunt's 'partiality for the Navy', the 'readiness and accuracy with which she wrote about it'; 'with ships and sailors', he says, 'she felt herself at home'.[2] Austen-Leigh was able to say this with the confidence of personal knowledge. He could also have said that his aunt was very knowledgeable about the naval events of this period. Her principal source of information – we would call it inside information – came in the letters of the sailor brothers, who wrote home with some regularity and regarded their sister Jane as their principal point of contact with the family. The broader picture she would have picked up from the daily and weekly newspapers, in which news of the war at sea featured prominently. Added to this, the Austens had a wide circle of naval connections, many of them friends of the sailor brothers and relations of the family through marriage. For example, Jane Cooper, one of Jane Austen's closest childhood friends, in 1792 married Captain Thomas Williams, who was to be an Admiral; and amongst the remoter cousinage there was a scattering of Admirals and senior Admiralty officials. This was the naval network that kept the Austens well-informed over the years with which we are particularly concerned – that is, the eleven years from the time of Charles's arrival at Bermuda in 1804, and Halifax a year later, until mid-1816, when Jane Austen finished writing *Persuasion*. These years saw the growing tension between Britain and the United States, leading to the War of 1812, a war which began as a war at sea, a conflict in which the naval stations at Halifax and Bermuda played a vital role as the only fortified naval bases securing British interests in the entire Western hemisphere.

Whereas Bermuda was a recent establishment, the Halifax base went back to 1749. It was the most heavily fortified overseas base in the British Empire, valuable for its extremely large natural harbour, capable of providing a secure and sheltered anchorage for a naval squadron and more. Strategically, too, it was of great importance in its command of the North Atlantic and the Gulf of St Lawrence. And with the coming of American Independence Halifax was the lone British naval base from the Arctic North down to the West Indies, a sweep of ocean upwards of four thousand miles.

Bermuda was a different case entirely. Since the time of its first settlement in the 1600's, as far as the Navy was concerned, it was thought to be of no value at all. It was remote from land and judged virtually unapproachable on account of the surrounding shoals and barriers of coral reef. According to the charts, nothing larger than a fishing boat could get through to the harbour of the main island. But that view changed in 1794 when a naval survey revealed a channel that was navigable by larger vessels. An anchorage was recommended to the Admiralty and a site proposed for a naval dockyard. A year later, it was realised that Bermuda could serve as a winter base for the North America Squadron. Fifteen hundred miles to the south of Halifax, it could provide a southern rendezvous for naval forces and could also be used as a staging point for convoys and their escorts continuing further southwards to the West Indies. In 1805, the Halifax Squadron began to winter at Bermuda for six or seven months, from November to May or June, headed by the Commander-in-Chief in his Flagship, and his Headquarters staff.

But the full strategic value of Bermuda was revealed only a few years later, with the War of 1812. For in its isolation and difficulty of access, it provided an extremely secure base, and it commanded the entire Eastern seaboard of the United States, including some of the vital waterways, Chesapeake Bay for example, exposing Baltimore and Washington to naval attack. It was for very good reason that Bermuda was famed as 'The Gibraltar of the West', just as Kipling was to call Halifax 'The Warden of the North'.[3] As history reminds us, these were titles well deserved.

With an eye to the future importance of Bermuda, a shore establishment and yards were developed. Bermudian sloops were admired for their fast sailing and an increasing number of vessels for naval use were built locally in the well-established shipyards. In this development Halifax was vital since Bermuda's native wood was cedar, which was expensive and only available in limited quantities. The Bermuda ship-building and repair yards turned increasingly to the timber resources of Nova Scotia, New Brunswick, and elsewhere in Upper and Lower Canada, and these shipments came to Bermuda via Halifax. Similarly, as the Bermuda naval base grew in size, it was from Halifax that the supplies of building materials were organized and shipped, as well as the meat and other provisions needed for ships that were out at sea for months on end.

It happens that the first of Bermuda's locally-built naval vessels – the *Indian* – was Charles Austen's. To muster his crew, Charles put an advertisement on the front page of *The Bermuda Gazette* for 13 April 1805. His description of the ship was cast in handsome, even extravagant, terms for a sloop of only four hundred tons and twenty guns. But in referring to its 'fast sailing' as a quality of its 'construction', Charles was trumpeting no more than the truth:

> The Indian is the finest and most beautiful Man of War ever built, and her construction puts fast sailing beyond a doubt. Therefore plenty of Spanish DOUBLOONS and DOLLARS will fall to the lot of all those spirited Young Men who come forward without delay … Grog and Fresh Beef every day at twelve o'clock. GOD SAVE THE KING, AND success to the TIGHT LITTLE ISLAND.

The promised rewards were forthcoming. Thanks to Sheila Kindred we know that in the next three years Charles was successful in capturing, on his own, or in company with other vessels, no fewer than thirteen prizes.[4]

Charles was also involved in the Squadron's routine duties, routine but essential. These included maintaining the blockade at sea, preventing American trade with Napoleonic Europe; intercepting the traffic in slaves between the British West Indies and the Southern states of America; escorting British convoys between Canada and the West Indies and between Canada and Britain; and there was the business of boarding foreign vessels, mostly American ships, to remove British crewmen, many of whom were deserters from the Navy attracted by better pay and conditions. It was Britain's enforcement of this right of search – a claim rejected by the United States – and impressment, a net widely flung that enveloped thousands of Americans (some estimates run as high as 13,000) which triggered the War of 1812. These issues were more than a matter of pride for the United States since they imperilled the success of its merchant fleet, second only to the British in size and activity.

But service on the Bermuda station was not always so demanding. Charles was a warm and easy-going man of considerable charm. Between his duties at sea, he found time to lead an active life in the upper circles of Bermuda society. He joined the select Freemason's Lodge at St George's, the 'naval' end of 'the tight little island' and mixed with the best families. A personable and successful young naval officer in his late twenties, and unmarried, he was regarded as a good catch. Fond of parties and dancing, to the matrons of Bermuda he must have seemed one of those single men who 'must be in want of a wife' (as Jane Austen opens *Pride and Prejudice*). In the event, Charles married Fanny Palmer, a well-connected young lady of 17, the youngest daughter of the island's former Attorney-General and sister-in-law to the island's Chief Justice. Charles was equally successful in his naval career. Promoted Captain in 1810, he commanded the Flagship of Admiral Sir John Warren, the Commander-in-Chief of the North America Station. The two men were on very good terms and Lady Warren and Fanny became firm friends, travelling together when the Admiral moved his Headquarters between Bermuda and Halifax.

Back in England, the Austen family was able to follow Charles's promotion and his appointment to the Admiral's Flagship. Service promotions and appointments were announced regularly in the newspapers; and more detailed news was to be found in the monthly *Naval Chronicle*. And then there were the letters home from the sailor brothers themselves. Although only a few of these letters have survived, we know that both Francis and Charles were regular correspondents[5] and that most of their letters were addressed to their sister Jane. Her practice was to circulate their news around the family. We see an example of this early in 1809 when she wrote to Cassandra, then staying in Kent with their brother Edward. This was to tell her the news that Charles had taken 'a small prize ... a French schooner laden with Sugar, but Bad weather parted them, & she had not yet been heard of ...'. Charles feared that as the vessel and its cargo were lost, there was no prize-money to be shared out. However, the 'real misfortune' (as he wrote to Cassandra) was not this financial loss but losing 'the lives of twelve of my people' – the sailors he put on board as the prize-crew, to bring the ship back to Bermuda – 'two of them mids', meaning midshipmen, who were only youngsters.[6]

This letter gives us a valuable insight into Charles's character – his essential humanity. We know from his log books and from other official papers that he valued the lives of his men above money – not, at that time, an altogether common attitude among naval officers; and it was something his crews understood and appreciated. Not surprisingly, Charles was able to keep discipline on his ships with an exceptionally low level of punishment. Francis was entirely different, a strict disciplinarian. In July 1813, the Admiralty administered an official rebuke for the excessive levels of flogging in one of his ships. This contrast between the two men belongs to a general pattern. Charles was open and forthcoming and, despite all the sorrows and horrors of war, held a cheerful view of life, whereas Francis was a man who found it difficult to share his feelings, whose manner and outlook were stern and unbending. Like their sister Jane, both men were devout Christians. But we know from their family letters that while Charles found God a god of love, for Francis, God was above all a lawgiver and the source of divine justice, a being who demanded obedience and delivered punishment to the sinner. These differences were expressed in the character of the ships they commanded. Francis, in particular, found no popularity as the captain of what was known as a 'praying' ship. On these vessels, the sailors had to watch their language, keep their disorder and drunkenness well out of sight, drop to their knees at the Sunday service and join in the hymns. It is worth considering these differences since they help us to understand how these men were seen and regarded by their contemporaries; how, for example, Charles and his wife moved easily in Halifax society and were made welcome, just as they were popular throughout the Squadron. By contrast, during his spell as Commander-in-Chief, in 1845-48, Francis was regarded as stiff and unapproachable.

Sometimes news of the sailor brothers travelled informally, by word of mouth, which is how Jane Austen was alerted in the Spring of 1811 to the possibility that Charles was on his way back to England. She duly sent this report on to her sister (again, Cassandra was staying with their brother Edward): '... Capt. Simpson told us, on the authority of some other Capt[n] just arrived from Halifax that Charles was bringing the Cleopatra home, & that she was probably by this time in the Channel –'. But this communication was made late in the evening, at the end of one of Henry Austen's convivial parties, with everyone in high spirits. Jane, somewhat dubious about the accuracy of the Captain's news, added a note of warning: 'as Capt. S. was certainly in liquor, we must not quite depend on it.'[7] As it turned out, her doubts were well grounded; Captains 'in liquor' were to be treated with caution; Charles was not back in England for another three or four months. But by the Autumn he and his family were home, regaling the Austens with stories of Bermuda and Halifax, his successes in the *Indian* and his experiences as Captain of Admiral Warren's Flagship.

*

Charles's return to England, and the interest of his account, may well have suggested to Jane Austen the idea of introducing naval characters to her current work, *Mansfield Park*, a novel she had begun in early in 1811, around the time of meeting the drunken Captain Simpson; and we know that she consulted both Francis and Charles while she was writing the novel, seeking their permission to use the names of their ships, including the *Cleopatra*, the very ship in which Charles returned from Halifax.

This leads me to believe that the portrait of the young Midshipman, William Price – eager, enthusiastic and open – owes much to Charles's own boyishness and charm. A further detail, of some historical significance, was suggested by Charles's service in the North America Command. This comes in Chapter 12, the scene in which Tom Bertram glances at a newspaper and remarks to Dr Grant: 'A strange business this in America, Dr Grant! – What is your opinion? I always come to you to know what I am to think of public matters.'[8] In the calendar of *Mansfield Park*, this scene takes place in the Autumn of 1812. So the 'strange business in America' must refer to the early events of the War, America having made its declaration in mid-June. These early events were dominated by the humiliation, totally unexpected, suffered by the British Navy at the hands of the Navy of the United States.

British historians often speak of the War of 1812 as a mere sideshow. But that was certainly not how it was seen in North America. The aim of the Republican 'war hawks' was no less than the conquest of Canada. Optimistically, they saw themselves before long dictating the terms of peace in Quebec or Halifax. On the British side, the War was initially regarded as no more than a contest at sea, its outcome a foregone conclusion. The British people entered the War thinking of themselves as lords of the ocean, and the Americans as no more than disobedient children to be taught a lesson. Trafalgar had fed the British presumption of success. But in 1812, things turned out very differently. The British ships sailed, one-by-one, to disaster. They found themselves out-sailed, out-manoeuvred and out-gunned. First, in August 1812, HMS *Guerriere*, a frigate sailing to Halifax for a refit, was captured by the USS *Constitution*. The *Times* was scathing, quite carried away in its indignation: 'Never before in the history of the world did an English frigate strike [i.e., strike its flag, lower its colours in surrender] to an American ... Good God!'.[9] Two months later, in October, the *Macedonian* was shot to pieces, also suffering humiliation, surrendering to its American victor, the USS *United States*; and on 29 November, the USS *Constitution* struck again, capturing HMS *Java*.

The pages of the *Naval Chronicle* were filled with these disasters. One correspondent described them as no less than 'a national disgrace'.[10] Indignant voices were raised in Parliament. Canning lamented that the British Navy's 'sacred spell of invincibility has been broken' and in the House of Lords the Earl of Darnley followed Canning with a further outburst of eloquent dismay: 'The charm of invincibility had now been broken' and the 'consecrated standard' of Great Britain 'no longer floated victorious on the main'.[11]

Alongside these triumphs of the US Navy, American privateers came out in their hundreds. Many of these were merchant-ships. Finding themselves prevented from their normal shipping trade by the British blockade, they turned to privateering. Equipping themselves with naval guns, and licensed by the US Government with letters of marque, effectively they became private men-of-war, preying on Britain's merchant shipping. They ranged far into European waters, enabling Francis to score a minor triumph. At the end of December 1812, following a chase of eleven hours off the Azores, he captured the *Swordfish*, a schooner-privateer out of Boston. As successes in the American war were then so few and far between, the Admiralty made a great song and dance with his report. His official letter, describing the engagement, was made public and printed, first in the *London Gazette* and then in the *Naval Chronicle*.[12] And Jane Austen was herself able to add to the celebration in her own quiet way, bringing his ship's name, the *Elephant*, into *Mansfield Park*.

But this was a rare success. Early in 1813, American privateers were along the coast of Portugal, harrassing and capturing troopships and supply vessels. These losses led Wellington to complain bitterly at the state of the Navy, and gave the Army a chance to crow over its rival service, an opportunity seized with delight, since hitherto the Navy had treated the Army with contempt. Wellington's complaint was well-founded. Since Trafalgar a mood of complacency had taken over. Naval efficiency declined – efficiency not of the spit and polish variety, but the effective discipline of a fighting force, measured, for example, by the speed with which ships could be brought to action stations, the speed of loading and firing the guns and their accuracy – all of these operations requiring constant practice and drilling but remaining neglected while the Navy rested on its laurels. And this was as true of the North America Squadron as anywhere else in the Navy. Added to which, the Squadron had suffered by its very distance from European waters, which the Admiralty regarded as the vital centre of operations. The consequence was neglect. The Squadron remained small and, for the most part, its vessels were elderly. It suffered badly from desertions and was undermanned, so badly undermanned that there were times when the full Squadron was unable to put to sea. Overall, it was in poor shape. Successive Commanders-in-Chief, Warren as far back as 1810, had brought this to the Admiralty's notice, but with no success.[13] This left the Squadron incapable of carrying out its essential duties of maintaining a close blockade of American ports, guarding the convoys of British and Canadian merchantmen, and protecting Canadian coastal towns from American raiders. There were even times when Halifax itself was vulnerable to a sudden strike from the sea.

These problems lasted until 1812-13. With the War increasing in intensity, the intervention of France was feared and it was this threat that persuaded the Admiralty that reinforcement was called for. Between July 1812 and July 1813 the Squadron's one ship-of-the-line (what we would call a battleship, with upwards of 64 guns) was joined by another ten; the frigate numbers were increased from six to eighteen; and the smaller vessels-of-war from sixteen to twenty-eight; and as the War continued the Squadron's strength was to rise even more.

But the first British victory at sea, in June 1813, owed nothing to the reinforcement of the Squadron, nor to a general improvement in fighting effectiveness. It owed everything to the drive and deep pocket of a single English Captain, Philip Broke, commanding HMS *Shannon*. Broke ended the succession of British defeats, capturing the hitherto all-conquering USS *Chesapeake* and towing the American vessel into Halifax harbour. It was a victory gained within the space of eleven minutes, thanks to Broke's expert gunnery, his highly-trained crew, and gunsights of great accuracy paid for by Broke out of his own pocket. Grasping at this first opportunity to salvage professional and national pride, the *Naval Chronicle* hailed it as 'the most brilliant act of heroism ever performed'. This was a success, it claimed, that put an end to America's 'short career of maritime glory'.[14] It was a success, moreover, in which the Austens had a particular interest. Twenty years earlier they had known of Broke as one of Charles's closest boyhood friends when they had trained together at the Royal Naval Academy, Portsmouth, and the two men's paths had crossed several times in the intervening years. In fact, Broke had vivid memories of Charles and wrote to him in 1824, recollecting him as 'such a good temperd sociable little fellow in our *evening tea party* at the Academy – that I always recollect you with pleasure'.[15]

Another sailor deeply involved in the American war and familiar to the Austens was Charles's old boss, Admiral Warren. He had left the North America Command in 1811 but was re-appointed in August 1812 and returned to Halifax for a second spell, this time heading the newly-consolidated command of North America and the West Indies. Francis also knew Warren, having served under him some years earlier in the Channel Fleet. He was not a man to be forgotten. Whereas over ninety per cent of naval officers were virtually uneducated (in the formal sense), having gone to sea at eleven or twelve, Warren was remarkable in having been at Cambridge, where he enjoyed a reputation as a 'dandy', a 'young buck' and a gambler, and was described, disapprovingly, as a man of fashion with an 'extravagant lifestyle'.[16] But Warren had settled to a successful naval career during which he won a reputation for tact and diplomacy and served as British Ambassador to Russia. Judging that he might now be effective in agreeing terms of peace with the United States, the Government sent him out to Halifax for a second term as naval Commander-in-Chief, with full authority, as 'Negociator', to treat with the United States. However, it was an impossible mission. His two roles, as naval chief and peace envoy were wholly contradictory. While he was instructed 'to attack, take or sink, burn or destroy, all ships or vessels belonging to the United States or the citizens thereof' (so including privateers), he was also required, in the interests of his peace mission, 'to direct the commanders of His Majesty's ships to exercise all possible forbearance towards the United States'. In the event, it suited Warren's nature to choose the quieter path. But the enemy was not interested in 'forbearance' and the Parliamentary opposition was quick to seize on the weakness of Warren's position. In the House of Commons, Canning complained 'that the arm which should have launched the thunderbolt, was occupied in guiding the pen: that admiral Warren was busied in negociating, when he ought to have been sinking, burning, and destroying'.[17]

In the event, peace was some way off. The war continued inconclusively for a further two years, with engagements along the Atlantic coast and on the Great Lakes, and a series of British raids aimed at destroying coastal towns. These attacks included the capture of Washington and the infamous burning of the White House and other historic buildings, a vengeful policy which embittered the Americans and caused dismay in Britain. Eventually, neither side could see any benefit in continuing the conflict. On the British side, it was a drain on military resources to little purpose, since the threat to Canada had proved empty and the British Government had no interest in territorial gain. On the American side, the British blockade was crippling economically and the Government was unable to sustain the nation on a war footing. And both Governments had to face vocal and ever-growing opposition. War weariness had set in and both sides were ready to see an end to the conflict. Peace negociations began in August 1814. These the Austens watched with particular interest since leading the three British Commissioners was a distant cousin, Francis's long-term naval patron, Admiral Lord Gambier.

Nonetheless, even in the Autumn of 1814, there was an undercurrent of anxiety that the American war would grind on for years, and on a larger scale than ever before. These were the gloomy predictions that Jane Austen heard when she came to stay in London with her brother Henry, a banker. The duration of the war was a burning issue for the Austens, as it was for all naval families. For with the American navy quadrupled in size, they feared that Francis, now safe at home on half-pay with his family, would be recalled to active service. So Jane Austen was attentive to the discussions she heard among Henry and his circle and she attached some weight to this pessimistic line of thought. His visitors included City merchants and fellow-bankers, so she was well-informed. Some of them held Army and Navy Agencies (as indeed Henry did himself, in partnership with Francis), managing the financial and personal affairs of officers serving on the American front. These were opinions to be taken seriously and Jane Austen set down her own thinking in a letter to Martha Lloyd, a family friend (who was to become Francis's second wife in 1828). In this, she reported the depressing outlook:

> '*His* veiw, & the veiw of those he mixes with, of Politics, is not cheerful – with regard to an American war I mean; – they consider it as certain, & as what is to ruin us. The [?Americans] cannot be conquered, & we shall only be teaching them the skill in War which they may now want. We are to make them good Sailors & Soldiers, & [?gain] nothing ourselves. – If we *are* to be ruined, it cannot be helped – but I place my hope of better things on a claim to the protection of Heaven, as a Religious Nation, a Nation inspite of much Evil improving in Religion, which I cannot beleive the Americans to possess.'[18]

The 'teaching them the skill in War' and making 'them good Sailors & Soldiers' refers to the British claim that the backbone of the US Navy was composed of deserters from the British Navy, deserters who were already trained seamen and marines attracted by the better pay and conditions and who, so it was argued, provided the skilled core of the American fleet. But Jane Austen was prepared to take the long view. Whatever might happen in the short term, she was ready to place the outcome of the War in the hands of God. Believing Britain to be 'a Religious Nation', she trusted, ultimately, that its 'claim to the protection of Heaven' would be answered.

Jane Austen set this down at the beginning of September 1814. Only a week later she was writing quite breezily to a young niece who was attempting a novel herself. '3 or 4 Families in a Country Village is the very thing to work on', was Jane Austen's advice; 'such a spot as is the delight of my life',[19] as indeed it was. For at this very moment Jane Austen was deep in the writing of *Emma*, of all her novels the most sunny, peaceful and idyllic, its mood of good humour and high comedy as far from the shadows of war as could be. What we see here is Jane Austen's capacity to insulate her writing from her innermost anxieties. Nowhere in *Emma* is there even the faintest hint of the 'ruin' that the American conflict might bring, nor any suggestion of the profound religious reflections which the threat of war could awaken. On this last point, the same can be said of *Mansfield Park*. The war is referred to, and the sailor brothers' ships are named, reminding us of the North America Squadron. The penetration of American privateers into European waters is also mentioned. Sir Thomas Bertram's return to England from the West Indies, in the Autumn of 1813, is across Atlantic waters infested with privateers as well as French vessels of war. Yet Jane Austen makes no attempt to depict the dangers of the voyage. Quite the opposite. When Sir Thomas sits down to tell the assembled household about 'the most interesting moment of his passage to England, when the alarm of a French privateer was at the height,' any hint of anxiety is dissolved into comedy: at this very moment, Mrs Norris 'burst through his recital with the proposal of soup'.[20] Very soon afterwards, William Price arrives at Mansfield, the young sailor home from the war at sea. In the recital of his war experiences, Jane Austen shields us from the raw truth; all graphic and horrifying detail is excluded. Her reporting is indirect, kept at a remove. We penetrate no further than the 'horrors' of shipwrecks and engagements, 'the imminent hazards, or terrific scenes', 'every variety of danger which sea and war together could offer.'[21] And once again Jane Austen dispels any lingering shadows with a comic touch: 'and even Lady Bertram could not hear of such horrors unmoved, or without sometimes lifting her eyes from her work to say, "Dear me! how disagreeable. – I wonder any body can ever go to sea." '[22]

The War of 1812 was formally brought to a close at the end of 1814 with the signing of the Treaty of Ghent. But the news travelled slowly and small outbreaks of fighting continued sporadically for several months, coming to a slow end just as Jane Austen was completing *Emma* in the Spring of 1815. In June came Napoleon's defeat at Waterloo. In July, he surrendered to a British naval officer and was carried back to British waters until a decision was reached about his future. On the 8th of August 1815, the very day that the London newspapers announced Napoleon's departure for exile on St Helena, Jane Austen began *Persuasion*. It was designed to be a morale-boosting novel, showing the Navy in its best light, recalling the glorious days of Trafalgar and St Domingo, those high points in the careers of Admiral Croft and Captain Wentworth. (St Domingo was a victory in which Francis had taken part). Such an uplift was badly needed. Since those early successes of the American Navy, in 1812 and 13, there had sounded a continuous litany of complaint about the lamentable state of the British Navy, criticisms that resounded in Parliament, in the press and in the correspondence pages of the *Naval Chronicle*: morale at a low ebb; discipline in decline; desertion a growing problem; the old fighting spirit lost; war-weariness throughout the service. So the complaints went on. One officer concluded that British 'ships of the line were ... unequal to contend with a disciplined enemy; they would have beat a French or Spanish ship, who were worse than themselves; but I will stake my existence, had an American line of battle ship fallen in with one half of them, they would have been taken ...'.[23]

As well as morale-boosting, Jane Austen also used *Persuasion* to show sailors in peacetime, naval men now in a civilian setting. She arranges these naval themes around the heart of the novel, the story of Anne Elliot. After much suffering and endurance, her heroine can at last glory, as Jane Austen puts it, in the very last lines of the novel, 'in being a sailor's wife'.[24]

The connection of this novel to the North Atlantic is three-fold. We learn that Mrs Croft has accompanied Admiral Croft on his overseas postings, and these have involved her in crossing 'the Atlantic four times', and 'never' to 'the West Indies', as she says emphatically. This makes her destination North America and its naval surroundings, presumably Halifax or Bermuda, to which she refers.[25] And Jane Austen may have modelled her portraits of Admiral and Mrs Croft on Admiral and Lady Warren, in particular the scene in which Mrs Croft gently guides the Admiral's hand as they drive, a little uncertainly, along a country lane. In naval circles it was said that Admiral Warren's wife held the reins in more than domestic matters – gossip that even got into the American newspapers, which reported 'upon good authority' that Lady Warren was 'expected ... to supersede him in command'.[26] And perhaps most significantly of all, no less than three times Jane Austen raises the possibility of a *future* war, a prospect that Admiral Croft looks forward to as a piece of 'good luck'.[27] Charles Musgrove sees it as a golden opportunity for Wentworth, a chance for him to add to the fortune he has already made in prize money, room to 'distinguish' himself even more.[28] But it is upon her heroine that Jane Austen makes the possibility of war work its most dramatic effect. In the concluding paragraph to *Persuasion* we are told that 'the dread of a future war' was 'all that could dim' the 'sunshine' of Anne Elliot, now the newly-married Mrs Captain Wentworth. 'She gloried in being a sailor's wife, but she must pay the tax of quick alarm ...'.[29] Jane Austen's connection with the North Atlantic comes to a close on this sombre note, reminding us of the author's deepest anxieties about the continuation of the American war.

*

Twelve months after writing the final lines of *Persuasion*, Jane Austen was dead, the novelist cut off in her prime. Her sailor brothers, however, lived on into ripe old age, Charles until he was 73, dying on active service, leading the British naval forces in the Second Burmese War, Francis until he was 91. After seventy-nine years in the Navy, at the time of his death Francis was its highest-ranking officer, the Senior Admiral of the Fleet. In the years between, the sailor brothers travelled again to these parts. In 1826, Charles was appointed to the Jamaica station, within the North America and West Indies Command. Travelling out, he called in at Bermuda accompanied by his second wife and eldest daughter, staying there for a month, renewing old friendships. In the Caribbean, he was proud to record, he was 'most successful' 'in crushing the slave trade' and in flying the British flag in support of the newly-emerging states of South America, Columbia especially, where he gave assistance to Bolivar.[30] As for Francis, arriving at Halifax and Bermuda in 1845, in the *Vindictive*, as Vice-Admiral and naval Commander-in-Chief, it was very much a family affair. George, his third son, was the ship's Chaplain; Herbert Grey, his fourth son, was his Flag Lieutenant, and he would have brought his eldest son, Francis junior, as Flag Captain, had not the Admiralty forbidden it. As it was, when Herbert Grey left the ship, his place as Flag Lieutenant was taken by Charles Austen's eldest son, Charles Austen Junior. This family entourage also included Francis's two unmarried daughters, Cassandra and Fanny, to assist in official entertaining. It was an explosive mixture. Thanks to a sharp-eyed young Lieutenant who kept a secret diary, we know that the 'atmosphere' on the ship was 'dangerous'. Cassandra, the elder daughter, bore the ship's name, 'Miss Vindictive'; and by the time they reached Halifax Cassandra had become 'the Mistress of the ship, influences the Adl. in every way, and in fact, I *imagine* will soon be Commander-in-Chief'. Such, he commented, were the 'evils of a Family Ship'.[31]

Once away from the family enclosure Francis could be fiery. He had an unflattering view of the Americans he met at Saratoga Springs. He thought the men 'had some vile habits, especially that of frequent discharges of saliva, and that without much regard to where they may be'. And amongst American women he found 'a sort of flippant air ... which seemed rather at variance with the retiring modesty so pleasing in the generality of English women'.[32] Equally, the people of Saratoga, having encountered this peppery English Admiral, might have observed, in the words of Randall Jarrell, that 'To Americans, English manners are far more frightening than none at all'. It must be said, however, that Francis made no pretence of socializing, either in Halifax or Bermuda or anywhere else. Where he felt at home was in the *Vindictive*, directing operations against slave traders and conducting gunboat diplomacy along the coasts of Venezuela and Nicaragua.

Nonetheless, on the dry land of Halifax the 'evils of a Family Ship' proved to have a silver lining. For it was at Admiralty House, Francis's official residence, that Charles Austen's son, Charles Junior, met and fell in love with a local girl, Sophie Emma Deblois, the daughter of a prominent Halifax family of Huguenot descent. Their marriage took place in 1848 and in the Austen tradition of large families, they had five daughters and a son, this last baptised Charles John, in honour of his grandfather, the younger of the sailor brothers. Remarkably, when this lecture was originally given, there were with us in the room two of Charles Austen's descendants: one, a lady, born Margaret Bernadette de Blois Stokes, and her brother, Patrick Stokes, the organizer of the Conference and Chairman of the Jane Austen Society, both of them great-grandchildren of the 1848 marriage and great-great-grandchildren of sailor brother Charles, one of the principal characters in this account of Jane Austen and the North Atlantic.

*

One person, sadly, is missing from the picture – Captain Frederick Marryat, the founding father in the great line of English naval novelists. As a petty officer of eighteen, soon to become a Lieutenant, he arrived on the North America Station in 1811, calling in at Bermuda and Halifax, a town which delighted him. Twenty years later, he set down his impressions in *Peter Simple* (1833-34), the book that made him famous: 'All sailors agree in asserting that Halifax is one of the most delightful ports in which a ship can anchor. Every body is hospitable, cheerful, and willing to amuse and be amused'. When the time came for departure, the ship's Captain was too ill to sail, a misfortune that had its rewards. 'But we consoled ourselves: if we did not make prize-money, at all events we were very happy, and the major part of the officers very much in love'.[33] In September 1812, Marryat travelled back to England in the *Indian*, Charles's beloved Bermudian sloop, his first command. Did these two sailors ever meet – in Halifax or Bermuda, or later, in England? Unfortunately, there are no letters or records to help us, only the likelihoods of chance or probability. What we do know is that Marryat admired Jane Austen. His first novel, *The Naval Officer*, published in 1829, was hastily written, with some obvious faults. But he thought well of it and four years later set down his hope that '*The Naval Officer*, when corrected, will be so improved that he may be permitted to stand on the same shelf as *Pride and Prejudice* and *Sense and Sensibility*'.[34] Perhaps wisely, Marryat never attempted such an improvement. He was not a writer for correction or revision. Rather, as Conrad put it, his gift lay in the realm of 'youthful glamour' and 'headlong vitality', achieved in the 'completely successful expression of an unartistic nature'.[35] This is writing that stands at a distance from the finely-wrought surfaces of Jane Austen, the artist supreme. But a later novelist found a point of contact between the two. In 'The Captain's Death Bed', an essay devoted to Marryat, Virginia Woolf expressed her admiration. While she found no masterpiece among his works, she recognised his particular genius: he 'can create a world; he has the power to set us in the midst of ships and men and sea and sky all vivid, credible, authentic, as we are suddenly made aware when Peter quotes a letter from home and the other side of the scene appears; the solid land, England, the England of Jane Austen, with its parsonages, its country house, its young women staying at home, its young men gone to sea; and for a moment the two worlds, that are so opposite and yet so closely allied, come together.'[36]

It is tempting to imagine that the coming together of their worlds was more than a figure of speech – that one day back in England, Charles introduced Marryat to his sister, the anonymous author of *Sense and Sensibility* and *Pride and Prejudice*, and that the two of them were able to exchange views on novels, the Navy, and the North American War. Could it be that the 'youthful glamour' and 'headlong vitality' of William Price transmit energies that Jane Austen found first in the young Lieutenant Marryat?

Acknowledgements

In the preparation of this paper, I consulted a number of librarians, archivists and scholars in libraries and other institutions in the area of Halifax and Nova Scotia, too many to list by name but all to be thanked. I am especially grateful to Sheila Kindred of Saint Mary's University (see note 1 below) and to Christina Dadford Simpson of JASNA who generously supplied me with a disk which covered much of my subject matter and triggered my pursuit of Marryat connections real and supposed.

Principal Sources

Novels of Jane Austen: All references to the novels are to the Oxford University Press edition, edited by R.W. Chapman, 1923 etc.

Sailor Brothers: John H. & Edith C. Hubback, *Jane Austen's Sailor Brothers* (London: John Lane), 1906.

Letters: *Jane Austen's Letters* (Oxford: Oxford University Press) third edn, 1995, 1997, ed. Deirdre Le Faye.

Southam: *Jane Austen and the Navy* (Greenwich: National Maritime Museum) 2000, 2nd edn, 2005.

Notes

1 I have to thank Sheila Kindred for letting me have the precise dates for Charles's visits to Halifax.
2 James Edward Austen-Leigh, *Memoir of Jane Austen* (1870, 1871), ed. R.W. Chapman, Oxford: Clarendon Press, 1926, 1951, pp. 15-16.
3 In the four-line poem 'Halifax', Kipling treats the town and port together as a pillar of Canada's naval strength, with its 'guardian prows' and 'virgin ramparts'

– the military Citadel which dominated the town and harbour and which no enemy ever penetrated. The poem ends 'The Warden of the Honour of the North, / Sleepless and veiled am I': in 'The Song of the Cities', *The Seven Seas* (London: Methuen), 1896, p. 13.
4   Sheila Kindred, 'Charles Austen: Prize Chaser and Prize Taker on the North American Station 1805-1808', *Persuasions* (published by the Jane Austen Society of North America), No. 26 (2004), pp. 188-194.
5   Although few letters have survived, based on the evidence of Jane Austen's letters it seems that while the sailor brothers were away on service there was a regular exchange of correspondence with their sister: from Francis a letter came every three or four weeks; from Charles somewhat less frequently.
6   Letter of 24 January 1809 (*Letters*, p. 80); Letter of 24 December 1808 (*Sailor Brothers*, p. 209).
7   Letter to Cassandra at Godmersham, 25 April 1811 (*Letters*, p. 184). Captain Simpson is almost certainly John, born 1766. He would have known Charles since he served in the North America Command at the same time, was Captain of the Cleopatra (1807-08) and known to have been in Halifax in 1809.
8   *Mansfield Park*, p. 119.
9   Quoted in G.J. Marcus, *A Naval History of England* (London: Longmans), 1961, vol. 1, p. 460.
10 *Naval Chronicle* (January-June 1813), xxix, 11.
11 Henry C. Wilkinson, *Bermuda From Sail to Steam: The History of the Island from 1784 to 1901* (London: Oxford University Press), 1973, i. 313; *Hansard* (18 February 1813), vol. xxiv, col. 643; *Hansard* (14 May 1813), vol. xxvi, col. 182.
12 *Naval Chronicle* (January-June 1813), xxix, 80.
13 The condition of the Squadron and the correspondence of the Commanders-in-Chief with the Admiralty are referred to in chapters 11 and 12 of Gerald S. Graham, *Empire of the North Atlantic: The Maritime Struggle for North America* (Toronto: University of Toronto Press), 1950, sec edn 1958. All quotations are taken from these two chapters.
14 *Naval Chronicle* (July-December 1813), xxx, 41-42.
15 Letter of 11 December 1824, quoted in Park Honan, *Jane Austen: Her Life* (New York: St Martin's Press), 1987, rev edn 1997, p. 378.
16 *Oxford Dictionary of National Biography* (Oxford: Oxford University Press) 2005, vol. 57, pp. 486, 488.
17 Debate of 18 February 1813, *Hansard*, vol. xxi, col. 642.
18 Letter to Martha Lloyd, 2 September 1814 (*Letters*, pp. 273-74).
19 Letter to Anna Austen, 9-18 September 1814 (*Letters*, p. 275).
20 *Mansfield Park*, p. 180.
21 *Mansfield Park*, pp. 235, 236, 232.
22 *Mansfield Park*, p. 236.

23 Quoted in Southam (2005), p. 270.
24 *Persuasion*, p. 252.
25 *Persuasion*, p. 70.
26 Quoted in Julian Gwyn, *Frigates and Foremasts: the North American Squadron in Nova Scotia Waters, 1745-1815* (Toronto: University of British Columbia Press), 2003, p. 142.
27 *Persuasion*, p. 70.
28 *Persuasion*, p. 75.
29 *Persuasion*, p. 252.
30 *Sailor Brothers*, p. 114.
31 Quoted in Southam (2005), p. 320.
32 Quoted in David Hopkinson, 'The Later Life of Sir Francis Austen', *The Jane Austen Society Report for the year 1983*, reprinted in *Jane Austen Society Collected Reports 1976-1985* (Overton: Jane Austen Society), 1989, p. 256.
33 Vol. 2, ch. 18.
34 Quoted in Christopher Lloyd, *Captain Marryat and the Old Navy* (London: Longmans), 1939, p. 239.
34 *Tales of the Sea* (London: Printed for Joseph Conrad), 1919, pp. 10, [5].
35 First published in the *Times Literary Supplement*, 16 September 1935, pp. 585-86; reprinted in *The Captain's Death Bed and Other Essays* (London: Hogarth), 1950. The quotation is on p. 44.

Insular Austen, Oceanic Austen: "Bits of Ivory" and Beyond
Peter W. Graham

"Insular Austen." "Oceanic Austen." These epithets are respectively meant to characterize the author who consistently zooms in on a circumscribed neighborhood and the author whose fan base circles the globe, the novelist whose readers include both purists who simply want to experience her books again and again and extrapolators who use those works as intellectual or creative springboards for leaps that land them far from where Austen ever went, literally or metaphorically. The crux here is a question of scale and proportion. How can Jane Austen be at once an intensely and intentionally insular writer presenting a narrowly particular time, place, milieu, and set of social situations and an oceanic writer whose novels invite all sorts of wider connection or contextualization? On one hand, there's the "bits of ivory," "three or four families in a country village" aspect of her talent.[1] On the other hand, there's the side that inspires scholarly post-colonial investigations of Antigua and the slave-trade, such as Edward Said's or Brian Southam's essays on *Mansfield Park*[2] – but the oceanic side of Austen also inspires diverse fictive or cinematic borrowings, extensions, or recontextualizations such as Patrick O'Brian's naval novels, or films like *Clueless* or the recent Bollywood *Bride and Prejudice*, or Helen Fielding's Bridget Jones novels and the films based on them, or Stephanie Barron's thrillers centering on Jane Austen, detective. Besides inspiring vastly different sorts of critical and creative responses, Austen's insular and oceanic sides also elicit various categories of readerly reactions. There are nostalgic, insular Janeites, residing in her native England and far beyond, who mainly cherish imaginatively inhabiting the microcosms of her novels – and there are other Austen readers who are inclined to value what's transcendent in her works, who like tracing the oceanic potential effects of her minute, particular suggestions – and of course there are many, many people who appreciate both aspects of her art. Austen's empirical approach is crucial to this issue, I think. Like Charles Darwin, she begins by observing with a cold, clear eye and honestly saying what she sees. Unlike Darwin, partly because she's a novelist rather than a scientist and partly because of her personal sensibility, she's not prone to explicit generalization from the particulars she's noticed and recorded. But her fictions – or her data, if we want to call them that – inspire others who are inclined to voyage farther from the shores of England than she is.

Whether they're novelists, naturalists, or –ists of other stripes, people interested, as Jane Austen notably is, in what the critic Raymond Williams memorably calls "knowable communities"[3] must set the scale of their studies with care. Too narrow a frame and one risks observing anomaly or unconnected detail. Too large a frame and the patterns formed by particulars are lost in a vista's vast sweep. The poet-artist-engraver William Blake, a philosophical and political idealist who also, thanks to his incarnationalism, had his feet firmly planted on the ground, voices the dream or necessity of linking great and small. The best-known lines (1-2) from "Auguries of Innocence" articulate his aspiration "To see the World in a Grain of Sand / And Heaven in a Wild Flower / Hold Infinity in the Palm of your hand / And Eternity in an Hour." Blake makes this point more abstractly in *Jerusalem* (plate 91, ll. 20-21) – "... he who wishes to see a Vision; a perfect Whole, / Must see it in its Minute Particulars" – and yet again in "A Pretty Epigram" (ll. 1-2) – "Nature and Art in this together Suit / What is Most Grand is always most Minute."[4] A visionary, Blake did not need to identify a pedestrian means of getting from minute particulars to the perfect whole. But novelists of Austen's sort, like naturalists and social scientists, are obliged to.

Austen's near-contemporary the geologist James Hutton explains in a passage from his book *Theory of the Earth* how to get the scale of a study right. He chose the isle of Arran off the coast of Scotland as ideal for his British mineral survey, manageable yet representative. Hutton began by knowing only

> that there were most eminent alpine appearances on that island, as seen from a distance; that there was granite in those mountains; and that there were, besides, in the island, coal and limestone. But these, in an island of that extent, were sufficient to make it a proper subject of natural history, and interesting as leading to the knowledge of the original constitution of our land. The island of Britain is a country too great for that purpose, that of Arran, considering its extent, is not too little.[5]

Hutton continues that a naturalist able to recognize Arran's mineral evidence as sufficient to lead to "the knowledge of all that is necessary in the production of the land, or the surface of the earth, as a habitable world" will find the island's small size a "manifest advantage." Arran's geology can be understood empirically, but the process doesn't end there. The island's fully comprehensible yet representative nature makes it what we might think of as a geological metonym. Thus systematic principles can be inductively derived from the empirically observed data in such a way that close study of Arran can serve either of two larger purposes: theory-making or theory-testing, in Hutton's words either "forming a theory to be applied to other parts unknown" or "trying the justness of a theory formed from the various appearances collected from the different parts of the earth" (p. 200). Recognizing, as Hutton did, when one has found a set of minute particulars that will lead, gradually and incrementally, to the perfect or approximate whole it represents in miniature requires the serendipitist's trained sagacity as well as the empiricist's clear eye.

These strengths, I'd suggest, are qualities Jane Austen possessed in a remarkable degree – and I'd go on to argue that they're the very strengths that give her novels both insular and oceanic aspects. For instance, *Persuasion*'s knowable community of Elliots, Musgroves, Wentworths, and their connections shows us larger truths about primogeniture, upward and downward social mobility, and meritocracy in the same way that the excavated bones of a single dinosaur can, seen by a trained eye and placed in context, radically revise paleontologists' understandings of zoological classes and orders. Like a biological taxonomist, Austen plausibly establishes a chain linking small social and moral observations and groups them in ever larger categories. Like a geographer, she discerns the archipelagoes constituted by islands and eventually places those archipelagoes in an oceanic context.

Though not an actual zoologist, botanist, geologist, or geographer, Jane Austen was an implicit classifier. Nonetheless, she didn't write about her own qualities of mind or her fiction-making principles in a systematic or extensive way. She recorded little about the novelist's art in general or about her own particular ways of practicing it. Apart from what's demonstrated in her literary works themselves, what we can discern of her values, precepts, and strengths as a novelist comes principally from her letters; and much of the time we are obliged to operate by inference when reading them. Austen's published letters have sometimes disappointed readers who hope for something loftier, more speculative, and more artful than the prosaic, detail-dense bulletins she tends to dispatch. Such readerly hopes and disappointments, though natural, are at heart unreasonable. Jane Austen lived the sort of life she lived, and she wrote the sort of letters she and her correspondents (by far the most prominent among them is her sister Cassandra) valued. That ought to be enough. We should not be disappointed that Austen isn't as aesthetically speculative a letter-writer as John Keats or as amusingly confessional yet artful a correspondent as Lord Byron, any more than we should reproach her for not having lived like Keats or Byron – or them for not having lived like her.

Austen's penchant for close, clear observation – the skilled naturalist's eye trained to scrutinize the details of whatever social island she finds herself upon – pervades her letters. A typical passage of observation occurs in her Friday 2 September 1814 letter from London to her friend Martha Lloyd, then sojourning at Bath:

> I am amused by the present style of female dress; – the coloured petticoats with braces over the white Spencers & enormous Bonnets upon the full stretch, are quite entertaining. It seems to me a more marked *change* than one has lately seen. – Long sleeves appear universal, even as *Dress*, the Waists short, and as far as I have been able to judge, the Bosom covered. – I was at a little party last night at Mrs Latouche's, where dress is a good deal attended to, & these are my observations from it. – Petticoats short, & generally, tho' not always, flounced. – The broad-straps belonging to the Gown or Boddice, which cross the front of the Waist, over white, have a very pretty effect I think. (p. 273)

This close attention to minutiae – amusingly analogous, one might say, to Darwin's fascination with the diverse and fanciful variety in breeds of domestic pigeons – indicates genuine interest. It also displays sensitivity to her audience's expectations, for one thing cherished by women living in the country, as did Jane Austen and Martha Lloyd, was current intelligence of what fashions prevailed in sophisticated metropolitan circles. But although Austen was skilled at noticing and transmitting such trivial details, her art does not endorse female (or male) preoccupation with fashion or accoutrements. Her novels contain little taxonomy of gowns or greatcoats, and when a character displays explicit interest in clothing or adornment, the trait is heavily ironized. Only the likes of dim-witted matrons like Mrs. Bennet and Mrs. Allen, shallow materialists like Augusta Hawkins Elton and Isabella Thorpe, simple-minded ingénues like Harriet Smith, and dunderheads like Mr. Rushworth with his "pink satin cape" for *Lovers' Vows* or Robert Ferrars with his obsessive concern for the design specifications of a bespoke toothpick-case display overt concern with the minutiae of fashion that constitute the substance of Austen's epistolary report. At the same time, though, implicit attention to such details underpins the framework of the fictional microcosms she describes. Any Austen heroine pronounced "elegant" must somehow attend to such matters, though her thoughts and words remain beyond the frame of the narrative.

Prosaic details in general receive this sort of double-edged treatment in Austenworld, where it seems that admirable characters have the material concerns of their lives well regulated and hence should be understood as having been mindful of them – but where publicly putting one's attentiveness to small details into words is nearly always presented as a laughable quality, most pronounced in the case of *Emma*'s Miss Bates, who's apparently incapable of stemming the flow of what Austen, in a letter advising her niece Anna Austen on novel-writing, called "too many particulars of right hand and left" (p. 274). Miss Bates reports accurately, but she's an unselective and generally unreflective reporter. When Austen records observed particulars, she does so purposefully and selectively. For example, she provides the full details of Fanny Price dithering over the ethics, aesthetics, and etiquette of wearing her brother William's topaz cross, Henry Crawford's elegant necklace proffered by his sister Mary, and Edmund Bertram's simple gold chain precisely because these details shed light on the feelings, principles, and motivations of all five characters. Austen dramatically renders the specific reactions Mrs. Weston, Mr. Elton, Mr. Knightley, and Mr. Woodhouse voice about Emma's sketch of Harriet Smith because these reactions constitute data empirical readers can use to gauge not just Emma's artwork but its various interpreters. Artist, model, and audience, all are gathered by Austen into a community of interacting individuals knowable to one another and to readers. These characters caught in the act of voicing their reactions to a portrait constitute both a tableau deviously arranged by Emma and a dynamic microcosm evolving beyond Emma's control and intelligible to us in ways beyond her ken.

Observations on fiction – Austen's own principles and practices or those of her fellow novelists – are much less commonly encountered in her letters than are the minute particulars of real life as lived by those people among whom she passed her time. Her clearest statements on novels and their composition appear in letters to members of the younger generation of Austens who shared their Aunt Jane's itch for fiction-writing. Letters throughout the autumn of 1814 discuss a novel being written by her niece Anna Austen, who was married in November to Ben Lefroy. Aunt Jane pays Anna's manuscript the compliment of reading it carefully and taking it seriously. She mainly offers feedback and advice centered on specific details of character, incident, motivation, and word choice. A few examples:

> We are not satisfied with M^{rs} F's settling herself as Tenant & near Neighbour to such a Man as Sir T. H. without having some other inducement to go there; she ought to have some friend living thereabouts to tempt her. (pp. 274-75)

> Susan ought not to be walking out so soon after Heavy rains, taking long walks in the dirt. An anxious Mother would not suffer it. (p. 275)

> Newton Priors is really a Nonpareil. – Milton w^d have given his eyes to have thought of it. – Is not the Cottage taken from Tollard Royal? – (p. 276)

> Devereux Forester's being ruined by his Vanity is extremely good; but I wish you would not let him be plunged in a 'vortex of Dissipation'. I do not object to the Thing, but I cannot bear the expression; – it is such thorough novel slang – and so old, that I dare say Adam met with it in the first novel he opened. (p. 277)

These specific criticisms display the insular Austen's overarching values – keeping faith with plausibility as empirical observation understands it, deriving details from real life, relying on fresh language rather than cant phrases. These values are not announced in general form but to be inferred inductively. Her first letter, of Friday 9-Sunday 18 September 1814 does, however, offer Anna two explicit principles:

> You are now collecting your People delightfully, getting them exactly into such a spot as is the delight of my life; – 3 or 4 Families in a Country Village is the very thing to work on – & I hope you will write a great deal more, & make full use of them while they are so very favourably arranged. You are but *now* coming to the very heart & beauty of your book; till the heroine grows up, the fun must be imperfect – .... (p. 275)

These remarks to Anna straightforwardly reveal Jane Austen's own general preferences – but interestingly, a close look at her words shows that one of those precepts has particularly close relevance to her current project, *Emma*. Throughout her novels, Austen's center-staging of unmarried but marriageable characters, with children relegated to bit parts and married adults to supporting roles, is undeniable. All her novels follow this rule, restated later in the paragraph: "One does not care for girls till they are grown up" (p. 276). Her avowed "delight" in working on the interaction of a handful of village families more accurately characterizes *Emma*, which she was writing in 1814, than of any of her other works. Nonetheless, the formula loosely fits all six published novels. *Sense and Sensibility*'s Dashwood sisters are uprooted from one country neighborhood (not to say village), transplanted to another, then taken on their travels to London; so theirs is not so much a chronicle of settled village life as a discovery of new places and people. *Pride and Prejudice*'s Bennet sisters inhabit such a neighborhood, but it becomes worth writing about at the very moment when characters from the outside world arrive to shake things up and, in partial consequence, the Bennet girls gain the chance to travel to other places (rural Kent, London, Derbyshire, Brighton). *Northanger Abbey*'s Catherine Morland, having just grown up, is dislodged from her village home and allowed to turn fresh eyes on the delights of Bath and the gothic charms of the novel's namesake country house. *Mansfield Park*'s Fanny Price, saved from urban squalor by being sent away from home, matures in a closed-off country-house world that for years seems to contain only two related families – the landowning Bertrams and the Norrises at the Parsonage – until death and debt bring new tenants and their relations. In *Persuasion* Anne Elliot's story, like Fanny's, involves exile – this time from, not to, a country-house neighborhood, with new experiences and perspectives contingent on Anne's re-situation at Uppercross, Lyme Regis, and Bath. Allowing for these variations, the theme of "3 or 4 Families in a Country Village" formula fits Austen's fiction in general. But *Emma*, with its densely, relentlessly detailed view of life in a populous village and its handsome, clever, rich, vigorous, but almost claustrophobically trapped heroine, is the best possible example of fruitful insularity as Austen the novelist understood it.

In contrast to her uninflected, highly particular advice to Anna, Austen's remarks of Monday 16-Tuesday 17 December 1816 to Anna's brother James Edward Austen, also trying his hand at novel-writing, seem arch, artful, and self-deprecatory. These remarks remind us that Jane Austen could be waspish – and she well deserved to be so when others, especially members of her family, failed to understand how demanding and difficult the process of novel-writing is when practiced responsibly. Austen offers her nephew an obviously facetious recommendation of plagiarism, particularly amusing in that it comes from a clergyman's daughter who never put a sermon into one of her novels and it goes to a clergyman's son: "Uncle Henry writes very superior Sermons. – You & I must try to get hold of one or two, & put them into our Novels; – it would be a fine help to a volume; & we could make our Heroine read it aloud of a Sunday Evening ..." (p. 323). One can't help but wonder if this whimsical suggestion doesn't contain an oblique slam at James Edward's father James, the eldest Austen son, who took over Steventon from his father and thus displaced his sister Jane from her settled home without intending to do so. Are James's sermons inferior to Henry's by implication? Is it a compliment for real-life sermons to be considered worth stealing by a comic-ironic novelist of Jane Austen's sort? In any case, James Edward's own style of novel must have been quite different from his aunt's, as becomes clear when she recurs to the matter of prose-theft, though in a different situation. She laments over her nephew's having lost part of his manuscript:

Bye the bye, my dear Edward, I am quite concerned for the loss your Mother mentions in her Letter; two Chapters & a half to be missing is monstrous! It is well that *I* have not been at Steventon lately, & therefore cannot be suspected of purloining them; – two strong twigs & a half towards a Nest of my own, would have been something. – I do not think however that any theft of that sort would be really very useful to me. What should I do with your strong, manly, spirited Sketches, full of Variety & Glow? – How could I possibly join them on to the little bit (two Inches wide) of Ivory on which I work with so fine a Brush, as produces little effect after much labour? (p. 323)

However humorously self-deprecatory the invocation of stereotypes – dainty, feminine Jane deferring to robust, virile James Edward – this passage has the potential to seem patronizing, perhaps even a bit unpleasant. Unless Edward were a pompous youth remarkably unappreciative of his aunt's published brilliance and even more infatuated than adolescent writers tend to be with his own apprentice efforts, he would very likely have squirmed at the irony. Over the years Austen's memorable metaphor "little bit (two Inches wide) of Ivory" has often been wrenched from its epistolary frame and read uninflected, as Austen's sincere self-characterization as a literary miniaturist. But the delicate balance of self-disclosure and misleading pose is what makes the passage worth considering and remembering. Insular Austen understands full well how limited and perhaps trivial her chosen field of fiction-writing looks from certain vantage points, such as those of romancers, philosophers, moralizers, generalizers, practitioners of what Sir Walter Scott called "the big Bow Wow" when comparing his fiction-writing talent, deployed in the genre of the historical novel, to hers.[6] But from Austen's perspective, that of the empirical novelist-naturalist, a small field's well worth intensive labour. A scrap of little island, such as the main street of Highbury, offering nothing more promising than a tray-bearing butcher, a tidy old woman carrying her full basket home from the market, two curs contesting a dirty bone (perhaps dropped by the butcher?) and a gaggle of children eyeing shop-window gingerbread is worth observing – whether by a self-described imaginist like Emma or an empirical novelist like her inventor Austen.

The blend of irony and honesty, self-deprecation and self-confidence detectable in the letter to James Edward Austen is more continuously and unambiguously evident in Jane Austen's correspondence with James Stanier Clarke, though the recipient himself, a man apparently tone-deaf to wryness, seems to have missed it. The figure Clarke cuts in his letters to Jane Austen seems uncannily like that of a comic clergyman she might have invented. In his role as Domestic Chaplain and Librarian to the Prince of Wales, Clarke had informed Austen that she was at liberty to dedicate any of her works to HRH the PR – and *Emma*, being the work then in progress, was duly dedicated to the Prince. Having gained his point – one a courteous subject could not decently refuse to grant the Regent – Clarke couldn't help offering Austen advice for subsequent novels in a letter of Thursday 16 November 1815. Without directly suggesting his own suitability as a protagonist, he asks Austen "to delineate in some future Work the Habits of Life and Character and enthusiasm of a Clergyman – who should pass his time between the metropolis & the Country ... – Fond of, & entirely engaged in Literature – no man's Enemy but his own. Pray dear Madam think of these things" (pp. 296-97).

Austen's reply of Monday 11 December 1815 should have been seen as an unanswerable rebuff:

> I am quite honoured by your thinking me capable of drawing such a Clergyman as you gave the sketch of in your note of Nov: 16. But I assure you I am *not*. The comic part of the Character I might be equal to, but not the Good, the Enthusiastic, the Literary. Such a Man's Conversation must at times be on subjects of Science & Philosophy of which I know nothing – or at least be occasionally abundant in quotations & allusions which a Woman, who like me, knows only her own Mother-tongue & has read very little in that, would be totally without the power of giving. – A Classical Education, or at any rate, a very extensive acquaintance with English Literature Ancient & Modern, appears to me quite Indispensable for the person who w^d do any justice to your Clergyman – And I think I may boast myself to be, with all possible Vanity, the most unlearned, & uninformed Female who ever dared to be an Authoress. (p. 306)

But Clarke couldn't drop the subject. He responded Thursday ?21 December 1815. Clarke's letter begins with some tactless bustling about *Emma*, remarkable given his previous praise of her work: "You were very good to send me Emma – which I have in no respect deserved. It is gone to the Prince Regent. I have read only a few Pages which I very much admired." Having admitted that he's not taken time for more than the merest sampling of the novel Austen has dedicated according to his suggestions and sent his way, Clarke reverts to directing Austen on what she should tackle next:

> Do let us have an English Clergyman after *your* fancy – much novelty may be introduced – shew dear Madam what good would be done if Tythes were taken away entirely, and describe him burying his own mother – as I did – because the High Priest of the Parish in which she died – did not pay her remains the respect he ought to do. I have never recovered the Shock. Carry your Clergyman to Sea as the Friend of some distinguished Naval Character about a Court .... (p. 307)

So goes the formerly seagoing clerical courtier's effort to elicit Austen's interest and direct her insular genius in a more oceanic direction. But he recognizes that besides offering himself to the provincial novelist as a potential model, he might also extend the use of his urban library:

> Pray, dear Madam, remember, that besides My Cell at Carlton House, I have another which Dr Barnes procured for me at N° 37, Golden Square – where I

> often hide myself. There is a small Library there much at your Service – and if you can make the Cell render you any service as a sort of Half-way House when you come to Town – I shall be most happy. There is a Maid Servant of mine always there. (p. 307)

The diction (especially "Cell") and the level of detail (especially the prim mention of the ever-present, potentially chaperoning "Maid Servant") are wonderfully oily enough to have come from the mouth of Mr. Collins himself. But they didn't, and unfortunately Austen's reply doesn't exist.

It cannot have been too crushing, though, for a few months later Clarke wrote to offer yet another idea that flatters his own consequence while purporting to serve Austen's novel-writing interests:

> The Prince Regent has just left us for London; and having been pleased to appoint me Chaplain and Private English Secretary to the Prince of Cobourg, I remain here with His Serene Highness & a select Party until the Marriage [of Prince Leopold to Princess Charlotte]. Perhaps when you again appear in print you may chuse to dedicate your Volumes to Prince Leopold: any Historical Romance illustrative of the History of the august house of Cobourg, would just now be very interesting. (p. 311)

This inspiration, as self-inflating for Clarke as it is uncongenial to Austen's talent, must have made her laugh inside; but she keeps a straight face – or at least what Clarke might take for one – in her reply:

> You are very, very kind in your hints as to the sort of Composition which might recommend me at present, & I am fully sensible that an Historical Romance, founded on the House of Saxe Cobourg might be much more to the purpose of Profit or Popularity, than such pictures of domestic Life in Country Villages as I deal in – but I could no more write a Romance than an Epic Poem. – I could not sit seriously down to write a serious Romance under any other motive than to save my Life, & if it were indispensable for me to keep it up & never relax into laughing at myself or other people, I am sure I should be hung before I had finished the first Chapter. – No – I must keep to my own style & go on in my own Way; And though I may never succeed in that, I am convinced that I should totally fail in any other. (p. 312)

Recognizing and acknowledging her strengths and limitations, Austen affirms her generic allegiance to the fictional species called novel – and her subgenre, the insular novel of domestic country life – as opposed to the romance. She most explicitly avows the value of the genre to which her talents are best adapted in a long digression found in Chapter 5 of *Northanger Abbey*, perhaps the most sustained example the novels display of Austen speaking more or less straightforwardly in her own voice.

The passage comes just after the narrator has reported that Isabella and Catherine "shut themselves up, to read novels together." It's worth quoting in full:

> Yes, novels; – for I will not adopt that ungenerous and impolitic custom so common with novel writers, of degrading by their contemptuous censure the very performances, to the number of which they are themselves adding – joining with their greatest enemies in bestowing the harshest epithets on such works, and scarcely ever permitting them to be read by their own heroine, who, if she accidentally take up a novel, is sure to turn over its insipid pages with disgust. Alas! If the heroine of one novel be not patronized by the heroine of another, from whom can she expect protection and regard? I cannot approve of it. Let us leave it to the Reviewers to abuse such effusions of fancy at their leisure, and over every new novel to talk in threadbare strains of the trash with which the press now groans. Let us not desert one another; we are an injured body. Although our productions have afforded more extensive and varied pleasure than those of any other literary corporation in the world, no species of composition has been so much decried. From pride, ignorance, or fashion, our foes are almost as many as our readers. And while the abilities of the nine-hundredth abridger of the History of England, or of the man who collects and publishes in a volume some dozen lines of Milton, Pope, and Prior, with a paper from the Spectator, and a chapter from Sterne, are eulogized by a thousand pens, – there seems almost a general wish of decrying the capacity and undervaluing the labour of the novelist, and of slighting the performances which have only genius, wit, and taste to recommend them. "I am no novel reader – I seldom look into novels – Do not imagine that *I* often read novels – It is really very well for a novel." Such is the common cant. – "And what are you reading. Miss ----?" "Oh! it is only a novel!" replies the young lady; while she lays down her book with affected indifference, or momentary shame. – "It is only Cecelia, or Camilla, or Belinda;" or, in short, only some work in which the greatest powers of the mind are displayed, in which the most thorough knowledge of human nature, the happiest delineation of its varieties, the liveliest effusions of wit and humour are conveyed to the world in the best chosen language.[7]

To produce a work demanding "the greatest powers of the mind," "most thorough knowledge of human nature," "happiest delineation of its varieties," "liveliest effusions of wit and humour," and "best chosen language" is a worthy task indeed. That Austen could see the novel this way says as much about her as it does about the form itself. Second- or third-rate novelists might fail in one count or in all of them – but a discipline that ideally makes use of such varied and important powers has to be solidly grounded, whatever its island. It's deeply satisfying for readers to explore such knowable communities – but equally possible for the adventurous to push off from so palpably rendered a shore in a theoretical, philosophical, or interpretative craft and to sail far on seas of thought. The destinations reached by setting off from the island base we can call Austenworld are various, but the insular laws Austen discovers and displays hold true in these oceanic realms. Truths "universally acknowledged" by marriage-mad Regency matrons in Elizabeth Bennet's Hertfordshire will, with slight or considerable alteration, preoccupy the mothers of singletons in Bridget Jones's cool Britannia. The shadow shape of Sir Thomas Bertram's transatlantic plantations is implied by the subtle lines that delineate Mansfield Park. Historical contingencies Austen knows and respects in her novels provide data readers of our day can interpret to draw conclusions on matters beyond her knowable communities. So if some readers cherish Austen's insularity in and of itself they can settle in, contented with the ordering dance of matrimony that invariably concludes her novels; but if her empirical observation of individuals in knowable communities *un*settles other readers, they can extrapolate beyond those endings, or view them as necessary fictions artfully implying their own artifice. Strange but true: walking Austen's closely observed fictive islands can give us sea-legs for actual oceans she never sailed.

Notes

[1] Jane Austen, *Jane Austen's Letters*, ed. Deirdre Le Faye (Oxford and New York: Oxford University Press, 1995), pp. 323, 275. Subsequent citations will refer to this edition and will be cited parenthetically in the text.

[2] See Edward W. Said, *Culture and Imperialism* (New York: Alfred A. Knopf, 1993); Brian Southam, "The Silence of the Bertrams: Slavery and the Chronology of *Mansfield Park*," *TLS* (17 February 1995).

[3] Raymond Williams, *The Country and the City* (New York: Oxford University Press, 1973), p. 166.

[4] William Blake, *Complete Poems*, ed. David V. Erdman (Berkeley and Los Angeles: University of California Press, 1982), pp. 490, 251, 513.

[5] James Hutton, *James Hutton in the Field and in the Study*, ed. Dennis R. Dean (Delmar, NY: Scholar's Facsimiles & Reprints, 1997), pp. 199-200.

[6] This phrase comes from a journal entry of March 14, 1826, where Scott mentions reading *Pride and Prejudice* for at least the third time: "That young lady has a talent for describing the involvements and feelings and characters of ordinary life which is to me the most wonderful I ever met with. The big Bow Wow strain I can do myself like any now going but the exquisite truth which renders ordinary common-place things and characters interesting from the truth of the description and the sentiment is denied to me." Walter Scott, *Journal of Sir Walter Scott*, ed. W. K. Anderson (Oxford: Clarendon Press, 1972), p. 114.

[7] Jane Austen, *Northanger Abbey*, ed. R. W. Chapman (Oxford: Oxford University Press, 1933, rpt. 1972), pp. 37-8.

Canadian and American Readers of Jane Austen's Happy Endings
Sarah Emsley

Jane Austen Therapy

Jane Austen's fiction is "a source of comfort and delight," in the words of Allegra Goodman, a young American novelist who recently published an essay about the experience of returning to *Pride and Prejudice* after her mother's death. She writes, "I was twenty-nine and had never felt so old. My mother had died of brain cancer soon after turning fifty-one" (143-44). Alone with her baby on a rainy October weekend in her house in Cambridge, Massachusetts, Goodman picked up *Pride and Prejudice* because her mother "had loved Jane Austen and because rereading it for solace was something she might have done" (144). Her description of rereading *Pride and Prejudice* in these painful circumstances is very moving: she shows how she came to understand the novel's brilliant combination of satire and romance, and began to value the work on its own terms, instead of comparing it with the darker moral vision of a Henry James novel. "Until this reading," she says, "I had never appreciated Austen's fairy tale so well, but perhaps I had never needed it so much" (144). She concludes, "I do not return to it because it is the best novel I have read, or the most important, but because of the memories and wishes I've folded in its pages, because on every reading I see old things in it. The novel is a source of comfort and delight" (145). While I don't doubt that *Pride and Prejudice* provided consolation in a time of grief, I do want to question Goodman's claim that it is simply a fairy tale. Fairy tales may offer some relief from the painful realities of life, but the happy ending of this novel, and other Jane Austen novels, offers something beyond a temporary escape.

Many of Jane Austen's readers turn to her novels for comfort or consolation in difficult times, seeking what may be described as a form of therapy in Austen's wit and her sympathetic understanding of the complexities of society. Without claiming that the concept of "Jane Austen therapy" is necessarily limited to North American readers, this essay surveys responses from a variety of American and Canadian readers of Austen, from Henry James to Carol Shields and members of the Jane Austen Society of North America (JASNA), to explore the therapeutic value of the novels. Some academic critics prefer to emphasize Jane Austen's seriousness in relation to history, aesthetics, or politics, seeing readers who turn to their favourite novels for therapy, rest, or refreshment as inherently less serious as interpreters of Austen's literary achievement, not just because they are not academic readers, but because they are in pursuit of comfort. Deidre Lynch suggests in her introduction to the essay collection *Janeites: Austen's Disciples and Devotees* that "a customary method of establishing one's credentials as a reader of Austen has been to regret that others simply will insist on liking her in inappropriate ways" (7). Is it "inappropriate" to find Austen's novels therapeutic? I think not, and my reason for defending this kind of reading has to do not only with my own experience of deriving comfort from the novels, but also with my conviction about the centrality of the classical and theological virtues to Austen's work (which I explore more fully in my book *Jane Austen's Philosophy of the Virtues* [2005]). The therapeutic value of Jane Austen's novels is deeply serious: far from functioning as escapist or fairy-tale fiction, the novels offer a vision of the theological virtue of hope.

It is partly the hopefulness of the novels' happy endings that inspires readers to look to Jane Austen for comfort during difficult times.[1] One American reader says that the endings are satisfying because "People get their just reward in the end. It's like coming back to the tonic in music." Several young Canadian women I know, including my sister Elizabeth Baxter, read Jane Austen during any and all times of crisis, major or minor. The preferred novels of choice? *Pride and Prejudice*, *Emma*, and *Persuasion*. My sister's favourite is *Pride and Prejudice*: she says she can turn to any page, any sentence, and it calms her down. With the other novels she tends to read specific passages, especially the endings. One of her friends always takes two novels with her when she travels: one new novel, and *Persuasion* for backup. In *Persuasion* it seems as if Anne Elliot's chance at a happy ending has already passed, yet even this heroine finds a way to be strong and hopeful.

One JASNA member finds the novels "incredibly soothing" – "like visiting old friends" – and says that she has "always found solace in Austen's ability to draw fine distinctions in the mores and manners of her characters." It's the sense of order in Austen's moral universe, as well as the happy ending of the plot, that offers comfort. Joan Ray, president of JASNA, invokes the therapeutic value of the novels in a recent letter in the *Washington Post*, remarking that "a dose of Jane Austen or even Jane Austen 'lite' (the films) is always good for you!" (C11). Another JASNA member remarks that she reads the novels for "reassurance (not escape)." She describes the hopefulness that the novels inspire in their readers:

> I turn to Jane Austen and her writing to remind me that decency, humor, and genius are humanly attainable and should be pursued. ... I don't feel that she is partial or judgmental, just matter of fact about treating others with respect and applying one's conscience in all human interaction. Her writing serves as a reminder, a realignment. ... It does a soul good!

For this reader, reading Jane Austen restores a faith in humanity and hope for the future, as the novels show that despite the corruption, mean-spiritedness, and selfishness of many or even most people, it is still possible and well worthwhile to try to find goodness in the world.

A number of people speak of the experience of reading and rereading Jane Austen when they are caring for relatives suffering from illness, or when they themselves are ill. Some have found that listening to recorded versions of the novels helps them deal with insomnia – not because they find the novels dull, but because the language is so soothing. Anecdotal evidence also suggests that several readers turned specifically to *Pride and Prejudice* when they knew they were dying. The energy and hopefulness of this beloved novel offer reassurance even in the face of death. One woman says, "I read Jane Austen for inner peace; it exhilarates me … it calms me down." That balance between exhilaration and calm is important; it resembles Goodman's point about satire and romance. Satire satisfies the critic in us, while the happy marriage at the end of the novel gives us hope that it is possible to find happiness even in a world full of satirical critics and cynics.

Jane Austen and Despair

Not all readers, however, have found hope and comfort in Jane Austen's novels. For Mark Twain – to take one infamous example – the novels prompted despair rather than hope. An icon of American literature of rebellion and freedom reacts to the polite world of Jane Austen with a violent aversion to the constraints imposed on conversation and action in her society. The quotations are well-known:

> Jane Austen's books, too, are absent from this library. Just that one omission alone would make a fairly good library out of a library that hadn't a book in it. … Every time I read *Pride and Prejudice* I want to dig her up and hit her over the skull with her own shin-bone. … To me, [Poe's] prose is unreadable – like Jane Austin's [*sic*]. No, there is a difference. I could read his prose on salary, but not Jane's. Jane is entirely impossible. It seems a great pity to me that they allowed her to die a natural death. … When I take up one of Jane Austen's books, … I feel like a barkeeper entering the kingdom of heaven. (435)

Ralph Waldo Emerson similarly expressed his disgust with Jane Austen's world, saying, "Suicide is more respectable" than the "pinched and narrow" life she represents in her fiction (qtd. in Favret 168). Even some of those who like Austen's characters and style aren't convinced that the endings of the novels are happy. I once heard a graduate student in English recount the story of her travels with friends who wanted to visit Chawton House to pay homage to their favourite writer; this woman, instead, insisted, "Take me to her grave!" – not because she wanted to pay her respects, but because she was angry with the woman who had married Marianne Dashwood off to Colonel Brandon. Like Mark Twain, she proposed to triumph over Austen's death. (How serious they were about this triumph is another question.)

Instead of dismissing Austen's novels outright, Henry James diminishes her achievement by referring to her work repeatedly as "pretty" and "little." He attributes Jane Austen's "little touches of human truth, little glimpses of steady vision, little master-strokes of imagination" to her "unconsciousness" as an artist: he suggests that she "fell a-musing, lapsed too metaphorically, as one may say, into wool-gathering" and later picked up these "dropped stitches" or "precious moments" (437). As with his attitude toward his female contemporaries in the novel of manners, notably Mary Ward (Mrs. Humphry) and Edith Wharton, he disdains Jane Austen as a "little" master (or mistress) of the field. (He, of course is The Master.) James compares Austen with other writers who have been fortunate to write novels that sell well, and remarks that she is "so amenable to pretty reproduction in every variety of what is called tasteful, and in what seemingly proves to be saleable, form." "I cannot help seeing her," he says, "as in the same lucky box as the Brontës" (437). It is a lucky box that, to some extent, he himself wished to be in as well. Yet he doesn't acknowledge his debt to the style or the plot of her novels, despite the fact that the outline of *The Europeans*, for example, is clearly related to the plot of *Mansfield Park*, as a sophisticated brother and sister enter the home and life of a less worldly family, and cause substantial upheaval in the emotional lives of everyone around them. James echoes aspects of Austen's novel of manners – in the focus on the intimate moral lives of complex characters and the attention to details of propriety (or transgressions against propriety) – without consenting to give his characters the happy endings, through happy marriages, that her works provide.

Like James, Edith Wharton also chooses to end many of her novels with refusals, renunciations, and deferrals, sometimes with despair. As in Jane Austen's novels, Wharton's *The Age of Innocence* and *The House of Mirth* are concerned with the choice of whom to marry. In both cases, marriage is shown in some way to be incompatible with happiness. Either it happens, and it is miserable, or it doesn't happen, and the characters are miserable anyway. Given the endings of such novels, it is somewhat surprising that Wharton and James are often viewed as the American inheritors of the Jane Austen "tradition." Elisabeth Lenckos, a JASNA member who teaches at the University of Chicago, recently gave a talk on Edith Wharton as "the American Jane Austen." And in my book on *Jane Austen's Philosophy of the Virtues*, I suggest that Wharton and James are two of the most likely candidates for the continuation of the tradition of the classical and theological virtues after Austen. Both James and Wharton are strongly influenced by Austen's acute moral sense and by the nuances of her style, and they do inherit the tradition of the novel of manners, but they reject the happy ending, especially the idea that a happy marriage *is* a happy ending. They are more likely, with George Eliot, to begin with a marriage that will probably turn out to be unhappy, and to trace the disintegration of the relationship between husband and wife.

Or, in the case of *The House of Mirth*, the heroine, faced with the choice of whom to marry, never chooses, and the novel ends with death and despair. One of my students last year, a freshman, read Emerson's remark that "Suicide [would be] more respectable" than life in Jane Austen's fictional world, and immediately saw the connection with Wharton's novel. He makes the excellent point that Wharton's heroine Lily Bart appears to choose death over the prospect of continuing to live in a corrupt world where it is possible to marry for love or money, but never for both. It may be arguable whether her death is actually a more "respectable" choice, or even whether Lily actually makes a conscious choice to commit suicide, but nevertheless, the ending of this novel points to the severe difficulty of finding happiness in marriage. Writing about Jane Austen's novels, Wharton sighs, "Ah, Jane, you sorceress!" She may be contemplating the wonders of Jane Austen's creation – but she may also be coming to the conclusion that Austen's happy marriages are magical in the sense that they are unreal. Edith Wharton and Henry James may have inherited many things from Jane Austen, but they did not choose to inherit the happy ending. Who did inherit it, if anyone?

The Happy Ending

In her Darwin Lecture at Darwin College, Cambridge, more than twenty years ago, Dame Helen Gardner set out to analyze happy endings, "and what has happened to them" (49). She attributes the "depressing cult of cheerlessness" in twentieth-century fiction to "the general breakdown of social bonds," and deplores the modern critical practice of deconstructing happy endings to show that they are always illusory (49-50). Similarly, Eugene R. August, in an article on "Divine Comedies in Western Literature," argues both that "tragic vision" has become equated with despair, and that "tragic awareness has been exalted into a kind of orthodoxy." Thus, he suggests, "the critical bias which sees tragedy as the highest art form" has "effectively relegated comedies to the status of second-class art" (87). If it is true that twentieth and twenty-first century criticism has privileged tragedy over comedy, it is no wonder that even the comedies of Jane Austen are sometimes dismissed as frivolous – entertaining, but not serious enough. August concludes by suggesting that while it is important to honor "tragic vision, we must be free to celebrate as well that opposing, or complementary, comic vision which discerns the potential for laughter and survival in the human lot. And," he adds, "we must be allowed to consider as something more than an evasion that vision of life which discerns the possibility of joyous reconciliation between humanity and a divine order" (98). An ending that re-establishes harmony should not automatically be considered inferior, especially if the work takes account of the potential temptations of despair, as Jane Austen's novels do.

The novels contain many references to characters on the verge of despair: for example, Edward Ferrars thinks "almost with despair" about the possibility of being able to marry Elinor Dashwood (*SS* 364), Jane Bennet is "almost hopeless" about Lydia's elopement with Wickham (*PP* 303), and Fanny Price is "almost ... ready to despair of being able to love or assist" her sister Betsey, a "spoiled child" (*MP* 393). There are only a few instances in which a character loses all hope. When Marianne Dashwood is ill and seems to be near death, the narrator says that she "could no longer hope that to-morrow would find her recovered" (*SS* 317). Elizabeth Bennet tells Darcy that she has "not the smallest hope" (*PP* 287) that Wickham will marry Lydia. Immediately after Louisa Musgrove's accident in *Persuasion*, Captain

Wentworth cries, "'Is there no one to help me?'" The narrator says that he speaks "in a tone of despair, as if all his own strength were gone" (*P* 138). When Fanny Price first hears of Maria Rushworth's elopement, she insists "'it cannot be true,'" speaking "with a resolution which sprung from despair" – a despair that leads her "from feelings of sickness to shudderings of horror; and from hot fits of fever to cold" (*MP* 439-40). These characters experience despair about illness, adultery, and trauma.

In the first three examples, the situation becomes more hopeful because the predicament is resolved: Marianne gets better, Darcy brings about the marriage of Lydia and Wickham, and Louisa Musgrove regains consciousness and health. It is only in *Mansfield Park* that the despair lasts longer. Fanny has "scarcely the shadow of a hope to soothe her mind" (*MP* 441), and "the unfortunate Maria" is ultimately punished by being "shut up" with Mrs. Norris (*MP* 461). Although there is no hope for Maria, Fanny's long-suffering hope for her own happiness is rewarded in the end: "Timid, anxious, doubting as she was, it was still impossible that such tenderness as hers should not, at times, hold out the strongest hope of success" (*MP* 466). While in other novels Austen shows how her characters fall into despair, and then rescues them with happy endings, *Mansfield Park* incorporates elements of tragedy as well as comedy.

With tragedy valued above comedy, what has happened to the happy ending after Jane Austen? Several Victorian novelists make use of such endings, symbolized by marriages, but, as Barbara Weiss points out in an essay called "The Dilemma of Happily Ever After," as the century progressed, these endings increasingly began to show a lack of confidence in the power of marriage to restore order. In the twentieth century, I suspect that the happy ending, in a way, went underground: it emerges primarily in children's literature and young adult fiction, written by such authors as, for example, C.S. Lewis, or L.M. Montgomery.

Divine Comedy in Children's Literature

To the extent that Lewis's "Narnia" books celebrate divine reconciliation after spiritual struggles involving both the classical and the theological virtues, they continue in the same tradition as, for example, *Mansfield Park*. However, they are far from being realist novels of manners. The work of Canadian writer Lucy Maud Montgomery, creator of *Anne of Green Gables*, is much closer to the characterization, plot, and happy ending of a Jane Austen novel. In the "Anne" series, which also includes *Anne of Avonlea*, *Anne of the Island*, *Anne of Windy Poplars*, *Anne's House of Dreams*, *Rainbow Valley*, and *Rilla of Ingleside*, the orphaned, red-haired Prince Edward Island heroine Anne Shirley (Anne with an "e") endures several struggles with morals and manners, and engages in a Beatrice and Benedick-like competition with Gilbert Blythe, her only intellectual equal in Avonlea society. Like Elizabeth Bennet and Mr. Darcy, themselves echoes of Shakespeare's heroine and hero, Anne and Gilbert argue for a long time before they begin to recognize that they are in fact deeply in love with one another. Each of the "Anne" books has a happy ending, although the marriage between Anne and Gilbert doesn't actually occur until the fifth volume. Their marriage is traced for several years, until their children are grown up enough for their daughter Rilla to merit a novel devoted to her story, and, while the marriage is not always easy, it is shown to be fundamentally happy. As in Jane Austen's novels, and in Shakespeare's comedies, the possibility of at least one happy marriage helps to affirm that there is cause for hope.

Montgomery participates in the tradition of the realist novel of manners as practiced by Jane Austen and she affirms the value of the happy ending. But she is primarily writing for a young audience – what about novels for "grown-ups"? Virginia Woolf declared that George Eliot's *Middlemarch* was "one of the few English novels written for grown-up people" (657). Was it the note of despair in *Middlemarch*, a distrust of the possibility of a happy ending for Dorothea Brooke, that led Woolf to see it as, at last, a novel for serious adult readers? In the novel's "Finale," the narrator says that "we insignificant people with our daily words and acts are preparing the lives of many Dorotheas, some of which may present a far sadder sacrifice than that of the Dorothea we know" (578).

"Anything Can Happen"

My last example of North American readers and writers on Jane Austen is the Canadian novelist Carol Shields, author of the Penguin Lives biography of Jane Austen, and winner of the 1993 Governor General's Award for Fiction and the 1995 Pulitzer Prize for her novel *The Stone Diaries*. This award-winning novel is certainly fiction for "grown-up people," but it doesn't have a particularly happy ending. After a long life of sometimes seemingly random events, Daisy Goodwill Flett dies, quietly but not peacefully, in a nursing home in Florida. It isn't this novel that I want to propose as Carol Shields's response to Jane Austen. Instead, while her early novel, *Small Ceremonies*, and her last, *Unless*, both share with Jane Austen's novels a focus on the small details of women's lives, it is her 1992 novel *The Republic of Love* that most clearly participates in the tradition of the romantic comedy with a happy ending, and the discovery of true love. Faye Hammill writes in her review of Shields's biography of Jane Austen that the plot of this novel "is basically the same as Austen's recurrent courtship plot. The orientation of the book towards the popular romance is also broadly comparable to Austen's response to the sentimental fiction of her day" (143).

It's true that *The Republic of Love* includes a courtship plot, a marriage, and a happy ending. The 36-year-old heroine Fay McLeod, and 40-year-old hero, Tom Avery, fall in love at first sight (two-thirds of the way through the book, and after years of being neighbors on the same street in Winnipeg, Manitoba, without ever meeting each other), and, after a series of hesitations and setbacks (Fay is afraid of commitment, and her parents' separation after forty years of marriage further undermines her faith in the long term chances of marriage), they do get married, and it looks as if they will live happily ever after. Before she meets Tom, Fay tries to cope with her loneliness by reading "One of the nineteenth-century novels she loved: predicament, resolution, a happy ending, always a happy ending" (158). After she meets Tom, she insists to her friend Beverly that she's having a "romance." Beverly declares that Fay is "far too intelligent a woman to be having a romance. Only deeply fluffy people have romances" (250).

The romance between Fay and Tom is not quite as close to a Jane Austen courtship plot as Hammill suggests. For one thing, Tom has already been married three times, and at the start of the novel, Fay is living with someone else – a man called Peter Knightly, interestingly enough. In addition to the complex sexual and marital histories of the hero and heroine, the courtship plot of this novel also includes a courtship so brief that it doesn't begin to compare with the lengthy conversations, disagreements, and reconciliations between Jane Austen heroes and heroines. Tom and Fay happen to meet at her brother's house one evening, he walks her home, she leaves immediately for a month-long research trip in Europe, and he is so certain that she is the right woman for him (at last) that he sends a letter to her hotel in Paris saying, "I love you. I love you, I love you. I don't know what else to say or why I'm saying it, but I have to tell you" (213). She, too, simply knows that he is the right one, and sends a fax saying, "I love you too. Returning home Aug. 31, 10:15 A.M., Air Canada, flight 192. I love you too" (218).

The Republic of Love is a romance, but these characters are not "deeply fluffy people," and despite the differences between their story and that of, say, Emma Woodhouse and her Mr. Knightley, Fay and Tom represent a similar kind of hope in the possibilities of romantic love. As Carol Shields said in an interview soon after this novel was published, she felt "a particular affinity with early 19th-century writers such as Jane Austen," saying that "they did understand the love story. They understood the importance of finding the other and weren't ashamed of it" (qtd. in Hammill 143). Although Tom and Fay are modern characters, and Shields's writing reveals a "postmodernist fascination with language and narrative" (Hammill 143), Shields defends the love story at length, as vigorously as Jane Austen defends the novel in *Northanger Abbey*. Fay realizes that most people, like her friend Beverly, do think that romance is "fluffy." She discovers, for the first time, "That love is not, anywhere, taken seriously. It's not respected. It's the one thing in the world everyone wants – she's convinced of that – but for some reason people are obliged to pretend that love is trifling and foolish." Shields writes that "Work is important. Living arrangements are important. Wars and good sex and race relations and the environment are important, and so are health and illness." Love, however, is seen as "something childish and temporary," something that "belongs in an amateur operetta, on the inside of a jokey greeting card, or in the annals of an old-fashioned poetry society. ... Just a love story, people say about a book they happen to be reading, to be caught reading" (248). (It's "only a novel.") Yet in spite of years of experience in dating and marriage that seem to contradict the possibility of true love and happy endings, Fay and Tom find each other, and aren't ashamed of "the miracle of it" (248). Love and romance may be miraculous, Shields suggests, but they are neither frivolous nor impossible. Sometimes, love does happen.

Early in the novel, Fay asks her brother what it means "to be a romantic in the last decade of the twentieth century." He replies, "'To believe anything can happen to us'" (35). This open-ended belief also includes the possibility that the "anything" that may happen to us will be bad luck, but it doesn't deny the hope that something good might happen. Hope, like love, is not frivolous. Hopeful people don't have to ignore tragedy and despair, blindly; instead, they may recognize and respond to problems while remaining strong. *The Republic of Love*, like *Persuasion*, affirms the value of hope, of second chances, and of the belief that "anything can happen" in the future. In her biography of Jane Austen, Carol Shields proposes that in *Persuasion* Austen "might be desperately rewriting the trajectory of her own life and giving it the gift of a happy ending" (170). Yet Anne Elliot's hopefulness is shown to thrive not just in happiness but also in sorrow and disillusionment, which suggests that Austen knew there was more to hope than the fulfillment that comes from a romantic happy ending.

Throughout *Persuasion*, Anne's strength and hopefulness sustain her. It is not (at least, not at first) hope that she and Captain Wentworth will be reunited – it is a more fundamental hope about life in general. Like her friend Mrs. Smith, she has learned, through suffering, to rely on herself, rather than on luck, to help her live her life fully. Despite her "cheerless situation" as a widow and an invalid, Mrs. Smith does not despair. Anne sees that her friend has an "elasticity of mind," a "disposition to be comforted," and the "power of turning readily from evil to good" (*P* 174-5). She herself exhibits a similar strength of mind in moments that come close to despair. When Wentworth cries for help after Louisa's fall at Lyme, "as if all his own strength were gone," Anne has strength and energy to spare, supporting Henrietta by herself while giving directions to Captain Benwick about helping Wentworth and about finding the local surgeon. Anne, "attending with all the strength and zeal, and thought, which instinct supplied, to Henrietta, still tried, at intervals, to suggest comfort to the others, tried to quiet Mary, to animate Charles, to assuage the feelings of Captain Wentworth" (*P* 138-9). Long before she renews her acquaintance with Mrs. Smith and is inspired by her friend's strength, and long before she begins to hope that Wentworth still loves her, Anne possesses hope and strength that enable her to comfort others.

The Republic of Love is not exactly like a Jane Austen novel, but it does echo many of the same concerns with hope, love, family, and the "small ceremonies" of everyday life. Perhaps it is Carol Shields, rather than Edith Wharton (or Henry James), who best represents continuity with Jane Austen, even though she does not write about the lives and manners of upper-class characters. The "Canadian Jane Austen"? Perhaps. (Although she was born in Illinois, and only later in life became a Canadian citizen.) It is a daunting task, looking for a twentieth or twenty-first century writer, on either side of the Atlantic, whose work may be compared with Jane Austen's. But finding writers such as L.M. Montgomery or Carol Shields may give us hope that the hopefulness of Jane Austen's work lives on in the novels of her successors, and that criticism need not always turn to tragedy for truth.

Jane Austen and Hope

A new novel called *Sex and Sensibility: The Adventures of a Jane Austen Addict*, by Rosemarie Santini, takes as its premise the idea that the love of Jane Austen's novels is an addiction. The heroine, Lizzie Parsons, is a member of a group called "JANO," short for "Jane-o-holics." Is reading Jane Austen for comfort, for therapy, a guilty pleasure? Like love itself, is the love of Jane Austen's novels something "childish and temporary," in the words of Carol Shields, less serious than work, politics, health, illness, the environment, and so on? Some readers of Jane Austen may be more interested in the lace, ballgowns, tea, and trappings of "Jane Austen's world" than in the moral issues raised in her novels. Yet for most readers, turning to Jane Austen for relaxation or "realignment" has a much deeper value. Other elements such as style and characterization may also play a role in providing "comfort and delight," but part of the attraction of the novels has to do with Austen's profound hopefulness, as represented by the happy endings in which love and marriage help to restore order in a corrupt and chaotic world. Her novels are not fairy tales, as Allegra Goodman proposes, and they are not the result of magic, as Edith Wharton suggests. Like Carol Shields, Jane Austen was not afraid of the happy ending, even in a world that thinks that the tragic vision is the only truly serious way to approach life. The theological virtue of hope is fundamental to her novels and she suggests that this virtue may be stronger for an understanding of narrowly missed tragedies. Life is fragile, but happiness is possible. Reading *Pride and Prejudice* or *Persuasion* over and over again is not necessarily an addiction, and it is certainly not frivolous. But you already knew that.

Works Cited

August, Eugene R. "The Only Happy Ending: Divine Comedies in Western Literature." *Bulletin of the Midwest Modern Language Association* 14.1 (1981): 85-99.

Austen, Jane. *Mansfield Park*. 1814. Ed. June Sturrock. Peterborough, ON: Broadview, 2001.

—. *Persuasion*. 1818 [1817]. Ed. Linda Bree. Peterborough, ON: Broadview, 1998.

—. *Pride and Prejudice*. 1813. Ed. Robert P. Irvine. Peterborough, ON: Broadview, 2002.

—. *Sense and Sensibility*. 1811. Ed. Kathleen James-Cavan. Peterborough, ON: Broadview, 2001.

Eliot, George. *Middlemarch*. 1871-2. Ed. Bert G. Hornback. New York: Norton, 1977.

Emsley, Sarah. *Jane Austen's Philosophy of the Virtues*. New York: Palgrave Macmillan, 2005.

Favret, Mary A. "Free and Happy: Jane Austen in America." *Janeites: Austen's Disciples and Devotees*. Ed. Deidre Lynch. 166-87.

Gardner, Helen. "Happy Endings: Literature, Misery, and Joy." *Encounter* 57.1 (1981): 39-51.

Goodman, Allegra. "Pemberley Previsited." *American Scholar* 73.2 (2004): 142-45.

Hammill, Faye. "'My own life will never be enough for me': Carol Shields as Biographer." *American Review of Canadian Studies* 32.1 (2002): 143-48.

James, Henry. Extract from "The Lesson of Balzac." 1905. *Jane Austen: Critical Assessments*. Ed. Ian Littlewood. 436-7.

Littlewood, Ian, ed. *Jane Austen: Critical Assessments*. Vol. 1. Mountfield, Sussex: Helm Information, 1998.

Lynch, Deidre, ed. *Janeites: Austen's Disciples and Devotees*. Princeton, NJ: Princeton University Press, 2000.

Ray, Joan. Letter to "Ask Amy." *The Washington Post*. 27 August 2005. C11. <http://www.washingtonpost.com/wp-dyn/content/article/2005/08/26/AR2005082601440.html> Cited 29 March 2006.

Santini, Rosemarie. *Sex and Sensibility: The Adventures of a Jane Austen Addict*. New York: Saint Books, 2005.

Shields, Carol. *Jane Austen*. Penguin Lives. New York: Viking, 2001.

—. *The Republic of Love*. Toronto, ON: Vintage, 1992.

—. *The Stone Diaries*. Toronto, ON: Vintage, 1993.

Twain, Mark. "Comments on Jane Austen." *Jane Austen: Critical Assessments*. Ed. Ian Littlewood. 435.

Weiss, Barbara. "The Dilemma of Happily Ever After: Marriage and the Victorian Novel." *Portraits of Marriage in Literature*. Ed. Anne C. Hargrove and Maurine Magliocco. Macomb, IL: Essays in Literature, 1984. 67-86.

Woolf, Virginia. "George Eliot." *Times Literary Supplement* 20 November 1919: 657. <http://www.tls.psmedia.com.ezp2.harvard.edu/member.asp> Cited 29 March 2006.

Note
[1] I would like to thank Elizabeth Baxter, Ryder Kessler, and members of JASNA and Harvard Neighbors for sharing their responses to Austen's novels with me.

Contributors

Sarah Emsley grew up in Halifax, received her PhD from Dalhousie University, and currently teaches classes on Jane Austen in the Expository Writing Program at Harvard University. She spent two years as a Postdoctoral Fellow at the Rothermere American Institute, Oxford. She is the author of a history of St. Paul's Church, Halifax (*St. Paul's in the Grand Parade, 1749-1999* and her book *Jane Austen's Philosophy of the Virtues* was published by Palgrave Macmillan in 2005.

Peter W. Graham teaches in the English Department of Virginia Polytechnic Institute and State University. His books include *Byron's Bulldog: The Letters of John Cam Hobhouse to Lord Byron*, *Don Juan and Regency England*, *Articulating the Elephant Man*, and *The Portable Darwin*, co-edited with Duncan Porter. A comparative study of Jane Austen and Charles Darwin is due out in 2007 from Ashgate Press.

Sheila Johnson Kindred teaches Philosophy at Saint Mary's University in Halifax, and writes in the area of argumentation theory. She has lectured about Jane Austen and published several articles in *Persuasions*, including "From Puppet to Person: The Development of Catherine's Character in the Bath Chapters of *Northanger Abbey*" (No. 20) and "Charles Austen: Prize Chaser and Prize Taker on the North American Station 1805-1808" (No. 26). She is a member of JAS and the Nova Scotia Chapter of JASNA.

Brian Southam is the author of books on T.S. Eliot, Tennyson, and Jane Austen, and has taught at the University of London. A former publisher and former Chairman of the Jane Austen Society, he is currently editing the Later Manuscripts volume in the Cambridge University Press edition of Jane Austen. His book *Jane Austen and the Navy* (2000) is now available in paperback, published by the National Maritime Museum in a revised and expanded second edition.